Miranda Ward is a writer. She was born and raised in California and now lives in Oxford. This is her first book.

Little Fish is an Oxford-based band fronted by Juju Sophie, an intense singer with the attitude of Patti Smith and the versatility of PJ Harvey. They've toured with Supergrass, Spinerette, Juliette Lewis, Alice in Chains, Placebo, Courtney Love, and Blondie, and their rousing live performances prompted The New York Times to declare that they have "the raw rock spark that doesn't depend on fame". Little Fish's first album was released by Universal/Island Records in 2010. In 2011 they left their label to pursue an independent career. Juju's new band, Candy Says, will release its first album in 2013.

F**k The Radio, We've Got Apple Juice

F**k The Radio, We've Got Apple Juice

We've Got

Apple Juice

Essays on a rock'n'roll band

Miranda Ward

unbound

This edition published in 2012

Unbound
4–7 Manchester Street, Marylebone, London, W1U 2AE
www.unbound.co.uk

Typeset by Bracketpress
Jacket design, cover and illustrations by Bekim Mala

A CIP record for this book is available from the British Library

ISBN 978-1-908717-21-4

Printed in England by Clays Ltd, Bungay, Suffolk

For Theodore Jetson Cassady Walker

Contents

Intro   xi

A very brief history of Little Fish,
for the curious or the confused   xiii

Preface   xvii

  I. Success   1

 II. Voices   13

III. Relationships   33

 IV. Value   45

  V. Doing It Yourself   69

 VI. Home   85

     Conclusion   97

     Interviews   103

         Laura Kidd   105

         Gaz Coombes   115

         Robert Rosenberg   125

         Ben Walker   137

         Juju   147

     Outro   175

Intro

I live in Oxford. I was in a band called Little Fish. Today, the streets are grey and fuming with rain. I shut the doors, undress and drag myself on to the bed. I lay back in the pillows, feeling grim. As life rolls through me in great waves I find myself thinking about everything that happened over the last few years. I was in a great band. We travelled the country, got signed to a major record label, flew to LA to make a fancy record and then toured the world with the likes of Blondie, Hole, Placebo and Them Crooked Vultures. I was supposed to be having the time of my life. I was supposed to be the envy. I should have been excited but I couldn't even get myself to react. So, what's it got to do with me if everything I worked hard for burned? It had nothing and everything to do with me. It had nothing and everything to do with the promises that the industry sold me. Music comes out of the air and hits you in the face like a last insult, and for all the good it does, I carry on. Don't let the wicked world get you down. We've all gotta live, like you and everyone else. Little Fish will show you how to love and to feel pain and as we pushed ourselves into flight, I thought, "is this what it is to be happy?"

– Juju

A very brief history of Little Fish, for the curious or the confused

This book is not a biography of Little Fish, but their stories are central to it, so it may be helpful to provide a little background.

The band has undergone a number of changes over the years, but the one constant has been lead singer Juju Sophie. Juju is the heartbeat of the band, the thread that ties everything together. She formed Little Fish and has carried it lovingly from one incarnation to the next.

For some time, Little Fish was a two-piece rock band, with Juju on guitar and vocals and Nez on drums. In 2010, they were joined by Ben on the Hammond. The following year, Nez made the decision to leave the band so that he could focus on his family. So Little Fish became Ben and Juju, who had also fallen in love and moved in together. For a while it was just the two of them, until earlier this year, when they recruited two new band members – singer Elisa and drummer Mike. They are now in the process of recording their second album, which they plan to release in 2013.

For the purposes of this book, I'm primarily concerned with the period of time between the release of Little Fish's first album, in the summer of 2010, and the establishment of their new line-up in early 2012. Events that occurred before and after this particular window do, of course, inform my writing and have naturally seeped into the text. But it was during those two years that certain crucial changes occurred, the implications (and causes) of which are at least in part what this book is about.

And so, for reference: a short history of Little Fish, from formation to the present day:

1999
 Juju's first solo gig

2005
 Drummer Nez joins the band

2006
 Juju and Nez record a demo

 Little Fish is featured on the cover of local Oxford music magazine *Nightshift* for the first time

2008
 Linda Perry – lead singer and songwriter for 4 Non Blondes and, more recently, best known as a writer and producer for artists such as Pink, Christina Aguilera, Gwen Stefani and Courtney Love – comes to The Wheatsheaf in Oxford to hear Little Fish play

 Little Fish signs to Perry's label, Custard Records/ Universal Motown in the USA, and Island Records in the UK

Little Fish record their debut album, *Baffled and Beat*, at Kung Fu Studios, Los Angeles

2009
Robert Rosenberg (Trinifold Management) begins managing Little Fish

Little Fish tour with Supergrass

2010

❧ Ben joins the band on Hammond

❧ Little Fish tour with Hole in the spring and Blondie in the summer

❧ Little Fish's debut album, *Baffled and Beat*, is released

❧ The band begin sending out handmade cards and booklets to their fans as part of the 'Little Fish Paper Club'

2011

❧ Little Fish leave Custard/Universal Motown

❧ The band record the album *Netherworld* with Gaz Coombes. They later send copies of the album to their Paper Club subscribers as thanks for their support, but it remains unreleased

❧ Drummer Nez leaves the band

❧ Little Fish release their single *Wonderful*

2012

❧ Two new members – Elisa on vocals and percussion and Mike on drums – join the band

❧ Little Fish tours in China

❧ The band, with a new line-up, begin recording an album in Ben and Juju's garage

2013

❧ Juju's new band, Candy Says, will release its first album

Preface

It was late winter in Oxford and I was feeling gloomy, so I went to see my friends Little Fish play upstairs at a pub on St Clements.

There had been a mix-up about the gig. I used to think that live music was simple: you had the people playing the music and the people listening to the music, and that was it. That is not it, as it turns out. There are agents and promoters and managers and press people. Sometimes they don't talk to each other. Sometimes they don't talk to the band, so one day the singer is walking along and she sees a poster with her face on it and that poster says her band is playing a gig tomorrow at 9pm in a pub somewhere, so they turn up the next day and play a gig at a pub somewhere.

I arrived late. The space was long and narrow, the walls painted black, the ceiling too low — one of these places that always makes you think of the very real possibility of being trampled to death by a mob, even if there are only five other people in the room. Ben and Juju stood on the stage — or, more precisely, Ben and Juju stood at one end of the room, which I took based on the presence of a few fairy lights and a microphone to be the stage.

It was just the two of them — acoustic guitar, vocals and harmonica. I've known Ben for a few years. He started playing Hammond full-time for Little Fish in early 2010; very shortly after, I remember him sitting on our couch late one evening, saying, but this girl's voice. You have to hear her voice.

I think I didn't really appreciate what he was saying, at first. I couldn't see what was so urgent about anyone's voice. I thought maybe he had a crush on her, maybe it was nothing to do with anyone else. I liked music, but I was wary of becoming someone for whom the whole world revolved around it, so I tended towards musical promiscuity – obsessing for one week over this song, then dumping it in favour of its slower, longer cousin the next week.

But he was right, I did have to hear her voice. I first heard it at a philosophy festival in Wales, where Little Fish had been invited to play. I stood at the front of the crowd, very close to Juju. She was holding a mug of tea, and she's small, but when she sings, it's like a prettier version of what happens to Bruce Banner when he becomes the Hulk. I watched her hair get matted down with sweat as the set wore on. It was late and hot and I was tired and had started out the evening resolving to be grumpy, mostly just for the sake of being grumpy. But I always know I like a band when I hear them play live and I start to smile even if I don't want to smile. And that night in Wales I started to smile.

And again, tonight, upstairs in a pub on St Clements, I started to smile. I suppose I always thought that a band came with a predetermined identity: that you chose your influences and stuck to them, that no matter how varied your songs were, once a critic had said you sounded like, say, "a cross between the Velvet Underground, the Spice Girls and the mating call of a kakapo," that's what you sounded like. And that may have been the case in some cases, but that is not the case with Little Fish.

I was always trying to come up with a way to categorize them, or a justification for liking them, but this was not so easy to do. I couldn't say that because I liked Belle and Sebastian or Bach I naturally also liked Little Fish. I couldn't even say that because I knew them as people, had shared meals with them, laughed with them, I liked them. I had heard them sound angry and loud and seen Juju look possessed, smash glasses, pour water onto the crowd; but I had also heard them, on nights like this, sound totally different; they tapped their feet, harmonized, hummed, like they were just in their own living room on a cold night, playing for some friends, or for themselves. Like there was a change coming.

Later, after the gig, we sat downstairs and had a drink. We sat for a while. We drank for a while. It's easy to become maudlin in late winter after a few ciders in a dark pub, and we very quickly became maudlin. This living business was hard, we all agreed. This making a living business was hard. And it was easy to look at this band, who made me smile even when I didn't want to smile, and ask them if they were crazy.

Are they crazy? Maybe they are. They've had to pirate their own album to give to fans in the US. They've toured all over the world, supporting acts like Supergrass, Alice in Chains, Courtney Love and Blondie, but at a recent gig in Leicester, they'd made £6.67. They didn't know how they were going to make another album, let alone a living, but even so, they were not going to stop playing music.

That night they told me about what was going to happen – or not happen – next. They were in negotiations with their label – a waiting game, mostly. It could go either way. Being signed was a Big Deal; it was the thing that so many bands, screaming their way through song after song, aspired to. But it was not the only thing: it was not necessary for existence. Maybe they would leave, go it alone. Maybe not. In order to fill the time now, in order to keep playing, they were recording acoustic sessions in a little flat in Headington and posting them online. They were making booklets of art and lyrics with hand-stitched binding and post-ing them to their fans. They were playing open mic nights in Oxford, which, I said to them, must have felt a little like a let-down after they had played the Royal Albert Hall last year, but no, they said, they loved it.

"Why?" I said. "Why do you love it?"

And maybe this book is an answer to that question.

I. Success

Now that Scotty has entered the realm of myth, everyone wants to own him. And maybe they should. Doesn't a myth belong to everyone?

– Jennifer Egan, *A Visit from the Goon Squad*

One night, in the summer of 2010, I tricked myself into believing in something that doesn't exist.

I'd been following Little Fish's progress for a few months by then, ever since Ben introduced me to Juju at an open mic night in Oxford. She hadn't been performing that night, just watching, but even then, before I'd heard her sing, I thought I saw what he meant: *you have to hear this girl's voice*. She was tiny, in skinny jeans and a loose jumper, and she sat quietly and sipped some juice and I don't know why, but you just looked at her and knew she'd be good to watch on stage. She was compellingly and objectively beautiful, but not in a way that made you think of insipid sex symbol pop stars; she had an appealingly gappy-toothed smile, slightly wild eyes, and there was an unpredictability about the way she watched and laughed. "Am I crazy, am I crazy, am I crazy, I'm out of my tiny mind," she sings on Little Fish's debut album, *Baffled and Beat*, and part of her charm as a performer seems to be her ability to convince the audience that she might very easily slip out of her mind, if she hasn't already. She gives the impression of being simultaneously tough as nails and vulnerable enough to doubt everything.

That March, Little Fish opened for Them Crooked Vultures at the Royal Albert Hall; the following month they went on tour in the US, supporting Courtney Love. I remember reading a review of the tour in *The New York Times*: "Little Fish had the raw rock spark that doesn't depend on fame." And my friend Ben, the web developer who wrote 12-second-long songs and had once flown to New York with my boyfriend and I and played a series of experimental gigs in office buildings, quit his job to be – well, what else? A full-time rock star. This is how I put it, anyway: I was always half-joking when I said it, but only ever half-joking. Part of me wanted to think that this really was the way it happened; you met a beautiful girl whose band needed a Hammond player, you said you happened to play the Hammond, and suddenly you were wearing beat-up leather jackets and being favourably reviewed in The New York Times.

By June, by the time they invited me to see them supporting Blondie at the Westonbirt Arboretum near Tetbury, I had begun to suspect that I'd wound up being friends with a band that was really going somewhere. I didn't think much about what "going somewhere" meant – to me or to them or to anyone – because at the time it seemed obvious that they were in the thick of it, rising stars just beginning to part from the cloud of obscurity, and this was too exciting a fact to be diluted by philosophizing.

I watched them play to a crowd of thousands outside at the Arboretum. It was the kind of warm summer day that England was made for. Little Fish came on as the sun, in its early evening descent, was starting to cast long shadows across the audience. They'd already played a festival in Cornwall that morning and raced to Gloucester immediately after, but they looked fresh; they knew that music was about hustle, that you made your own energy, and their performance was faultless. I was proud: I thought, I know these guys! And when they're famous, I will still know them, we will still be friends, we'll still hang out and drink beer and coffee and laugh about the world, but everything will be different, too. This was the moment: the climax of the make-believe story about music that I'd told myself, the dizzy instant in which I was so sure that everything was going to end like a film – in fame and fortune – I'd have bet on it.

Later, after the sun had set and we'd had a beer backstage, I sat with Juju in the photographer's pit, wearing earplugs to hear the music better. Above me, a few feet away from my face, Debbie Harry was gyrating in a kilt and a white wig, singing Maria. She held the microphone up to the audience, and 6,000 voices responded. And we were part of it, but also apart from it: we were here, at the base of the stage, intimate with the beat of the drums and the tap of Debbie Harry's boots, and they were all out there, on the other side of the fence.

After the gig we got a lift back to Oxford in the Little Fish tour van. The sound guy was driving – just a kid, younger than me, barely in his twenties, I think. The traffic trying to get out of the field where everyone had parked was bad; there was only one road, a long strip of white dust, and we were all on it, all 6,000 of us. It took us maybe an hour to get away from the field and onto the motorway. In the meantime I had a cider, looked around, at the mess: the detritus, a swimsuit on the floor, a bra on the table, empty sandwich boxes, empty bottles of alcoholic ginger beer. Juju shared a beer with Ben; drummer Nez talked fast, a long stream of stories, tilting a can of cider back, at one point opening the sliding door of the van and urinating into the grass as we crawled along at snail-speed. I fell almost-asleep, woke to discover we were at a petrol station, which we'd staggered into to make some brief but crucial repair to the van. Later, when we'd got back to Oxford, in the early hours of the next morning, I stopped for a chicken kebab with Ben and Juju before going home and falling heavily asleep.

The rock'n'roll myth, surely, belongs to the musicians, not to me: I never wanted to be a musician, never wanted the rock star life, the fame, the fortune, the tortuous, glorious ascent. I once played the violin so badly that a man paid me not to busk.

But there I was, in the back of a crumbling van at midnight, my hand closed around an empty can, my eyes closing in the warmth, basking in the aftermath of too much sun and sound. And I was thinking: *there is nothing glamorous about any of this, but it's the most glamorous thing that's ever happened to me.* Nothing had even happened to me; I'd woken up, gone to a gig, gotten a lift home. But I was thinking how exactly like a grungy little fairy tale it was: how exactly like you imagine it to be if you're following an up-and-coming band on tour, a real *Almost Famous* moment. I wanted this to be true for them, for my friends, for the people whose music I enjoyed and admired – but I also wanted it to be true for myself. I wanted to be part of it, even if I was just on the periphery, even if I was just looking in, looking up. I wanted to touch the sun too, in my own way, fly with my wax wings.

So, yes, their myth, but my myth too: everyone's myth.

❧

Gradually I got to know Little Fish pretty well; I got to know their life as a band, the convoluted logistics of it, and a little of their lives as individuals, too. I formed opinions; I learned that the sound I liked best, for instance, was not the mighty rock three-piece playing to 6,000 Blondie fans, but Ben and Juju, standing at the front of a room playing a short acoustic set to a bunch of half-drunk friends.

It turns out that singing songs to a big crowd is not necessarily a way to make a living, or even an impact: people are cheap, forgetful, and the politics of the music industry are oppressive (just because you recorded an album, for instance, doesn't mean you can sell it, or even get your hands on a copy of it).

It turns out too, that "going somewhere" is not a real thing, not even a state of mind. If you're going somewhere, where are you trying to get to? What will you do when you get there – and will you even know you're there? The bar keeps moving: first it's just getting a gig, then it's supporting someone big, then it's being someone big in your own right, and then what? Eventually, surely, the ultimate prize becomes not being famous, becomes regaining some of the dignity and privacy that you so happily shed all those years ago, retreating from the place that once seemed so important to get to.

Imagine you're young, you've formed a band. You start out in your parents' basement, say, or in a garage, in the school music rooms after hours, wherever you can bang your drums uninterrupted, wherever works. And you're driven by the desire for the attention of your fellow humans, the pleasure of having both a creative impulse and an outlet for it, but also by something else, something more sinister: a desire to be a rock star.

There's a basic framework, an understanding of the order in which things should happen. Because other people's lives so often look straight-forward from the outside, it seems reasonable that to attain what they have is as possible for you as it is for anyone else. Work hard, play hard, party hard, and someone will find you and sign you and then you will have made it. You will enjoy the support of your label. You will write a hit. You will get played on Radio 1, sell out a big venue in a big city, sell out according to your fans, be adored and ridiculed, rich enough, good enough.

Except that music is not a video game, with a set of objectives, an obvious ending point. You can't win at music. It's a livelihood, in the same dull way that accountancy is a livelihood; it's an escape, a form of entertainment, a form of art, a consolation, a reminder of things past, a presage of things to come. Occasionally, but only occasionally, it's a path to fame. Nothing is guaranteed.

One day, after I had been writing about and thinking about this thing called "the rock'n'roll myth" for a while, without having a particular definition in mind, I asked Ben what it meant to him. I figured it might be different for everyone, even if the foundations (desire for progress, success) are the same.

"The rock'n'roll myth is what everybody thinks the music industry is like," he told me. "It's what makes bands aspire to be rock stars and why fans have posters of bands on their walls. It's the musical version of the American dream." In other words, an invisible driving force, a (false) promise, a pied piper.

Of course, nobody thinks the rock'n'roll myth is going to pan out for everybody (though maybe everybody thinks it's going to pan out for them). It could happen to anyone, but it can't happen to everyone. Without striving, without winning, beating the competition, coming out on top, the rewards would be tainted by the knowledge that nothing was sacrificed or overcome to earn this prize – the prize would not, in fact, have been earned at all.

How often are we told that if we work hard, something will, or at least can, come of it? The advice of those who are richer, bigger, better, is always to work harder, sleep less, follow your heart: generic advice, advice that's only ever offered in surprised retrospect, as a kind of solace. By some accident of fate, I am here and you are there; you can be here, too, you can be a celebrity idol, if you want it enough, work hard enough for it: I have to believe this in order to justify my own place, so I need you to believe it also, in order to reinforce my justification.

And so the myth feeds its own hungry self, and the hungry myth depends on a certain shared definition of success. Look at it this way: when I was a little girl, I announced to anyone who would listen that I wanted to be a writer. I never said that I wanted to be a famous writer, but only because in my head, there was no distinction: of course I wanted to be a famous writer; all writers were famous, and if you weren't famous, if you weren't read, you weren't really a writer. Wasn't that how it worked? I imagined winning prizes, writing best-sellers: it seemed obvious to me that success was measured at least in part by this kind of achievement.

And why not? Why not think this way? The alternative seems to be to embrace the inevitability of failure, which renders any task almost impossible: why write even a sentence, when the book is doomed to go unread? Why play even a chord to an empty room? If you play a chord and no one hears it, did you even really play it? After all, music, like so many things, is changed by participation and reaction; it comes alive when people listen.

Little Fish have lived the dream. They've been signed to a major record label, flown all around the world. But if we assume the goal is fame, or some version of it, they're a failure: they're not on the cover of *Rolling Stone*, they don't even always know how to make ends meet.

But failure, fame: they're two empty extremes. And the question we now find ourselves asking, my friends and I, is what the space between failure and fame is, and why that space is not a more desirable one to inhabit. The rock'n'roll myth, the myth that makes music about some imaginary destination, is fallacious, even dangerous. We'll always have rock stars, or their equivalent. But success doesn't depend on becoming one of them.

❦

I had a moment of terrible clarity one evening in November. The weather had begun to turn, the days had begun to shrink. If history was any indicator, I should have been miserable – the cold, the dark, the endless stream of bills. And I was miserable, in a mild, ordinary way; I had not paid rent this month, I was not opening any post in the hope that if I ignored the letters from the bank the letters from the bank would simply not exist anymore, I was missing the feel of the sun on my face and anticipating the long grey months ahead.

But all of this was largely irrelevant, because I'd had one of the most satisfying days in recent (and not so recent) memory. I had spent the day – a good, full day, a solid eight or nine hours – writing (by which I mean the things around writing as much as the writing itself – making tea, reading, hanging the laundry, pacing the hallways). At about 7pm, I had stopped work and gone for a long swim. Later, I had a glass of wine and dinner with my boyfriend and we sat on the couch in the living room and watched old episodes of *The West Wing*.

As we were sitting there, in this suburban terraced house, it occurred to me that the myth is backwards. I don't want to be a famous author for the fame; I want to be a famous author so that I can structure all of – or as many as can be considered reasonable – my days like this. Because this, the writing and the swimming making up the bulk of my working day, is what makes me happy. I don't want to do that so that I can achieve prominence, I want to achieve prominence so that I can do that.

But the terrible thing about this terrible clarity was the associated disappointment: ambition, I had always been taught, or perhaps had taught myself, is crucial, and to admit that I don't want prominence for prominence's sake is to admit a kind of lack of ambition, or at least to admit an utterly selfish ambition. Success was not a big house and a collection of glowing reviews, though it might have been those things, though I would certainly not *object* to those things – it was independent of those things. It was only those things if those things were related to me being able to spend my time in the way I wanted. I wanted an audience, too, oh, sure, and there were lots of other factors – vanity, pride, insecurity. It wasn't that this was The Great Truth, just that it was another, and appealingly honest, way of looking at things.

"All I wanted was a chance to do the work I felt I had it in me to do," Paul Auster writes in *Hand to Mouth*, a chronicle of his own early struggles and failures. And maybe that's it: to want a chance to do something for the sake of doing it, not for the sake of what might or might not happen after you've done it.

❤

One night in December, a year and a half after I saw Little Fish support Blondie, I went to see them support a friend of theirs, ex-Supergrass frontman Gaz Coombes, who was previewing material from his upcoming solo album.

To say things had changed for Little Fish would be factually accurate, but too small a statement, really, to capture all of what had happened. Little Fish was born as a two-piece band – Juju and Nez, guitar, vocals and drums. The addition of Ben on Hammond had briefly transformed them into a three-piece, but now it was just two of them again. Nez had been forced to confront the reality of being in a band that wasn't making any money while trying to support a wife and child and pay a mortgage, and had made a difficult decision, one of the hardest sorts of decisions to make. Sometimes one thing you love needs you more than the other thing you love. The departure of Little Fish's beloved drummer was not technically crippling: their sound could evolve to accommodate the lack of Nez, to absorb it, create something new and good out of it. But it was a sobering thing, an ugly sort of reminder that the line between sustainable and unsustainable is sometimes invisible; it's possible to wake up one morning and realize you've inadvertently crossed it.

The band had also left their label, Custard/Universal Motown in the USA and Island Records in the UK, in order to pursue an independent career. The label couldn't offer them what they wanted, so they were going to see if they could get it on their own. Ben and Juju had moved in together, into a funny little bungalow with a garage they wanted to turn into a recording studio. These days we talked a lot about the music industry, and about the desire to make things – a desire that sometimes seemed irreconcilable with the logistics of living.

It was a small gig, in an outbuilding of a house that used to belong to Graham Greene's widow. The building was circular, two stories tall, but tiny. I had heard people describe gigs here as being "intense", which until now had seemed histrionic. But I could see the possibility for intensity: the audience had the choice of sitting downstairs, practically in the laps of the performers, absorbing their sweat and spit, or upstairs, looking down like gods upon the whole situation.

I went upstairs, to stand above and behind the performers. It was as if I could see exactly what they could see (the audience, eyes flitting, serene drugged-out smiles, half-asleep nods, toes tapping) but not exactly the way they could see it (I had the advantage of height). I tried to take arty photos from my arty angle, to consider what new perspective on performance this new point of view gave me, but I was trying too hard, and nothing interesting occurred to me, and none of my photos turned out. After a little while I went to the bar to get a mug of mulled wine. I looked down; Ben was moving microphones around, Juju was propping up a guitar.

"Don't spill your tea on the band," someone said to me, in passing, laughing, but I could suddenly imagine the disaster unfolding: the cup slipping from my hand, the crash of ceramic and wine, a song interrupted, the eyes of the audience turning to me in the dark.

"No," I agreed, taking a step back, taking the whole thing very seriously, "I won't."

The place warmed up slowly but noticeably. I removed my coat, my scarf. I stepped forward again, leaned against the railing: to hell with it, if I dropped my mug I dropped my mug.

"She's going to be a star," the man next to me was telling his friend, nodding at Juju. "I've known her since the beginning and I've always said that: she's going to be a star."

The set began with Juju upstairs, amongst the audience, singing alone. She made her way downstairs, down the spiral staircase, came to rest next to the piano. It was a good trick: you could see people turning their heads when her first note sounded, hear the smiles and the whispers.

On about the third song Juju lost her voice at the chorus; there was a crack and then a silence, filled, after a minute, by Ben. I had some time to wonder if the anxiety I felt was related to how vulnerable Juju looked from up here, how small and mild. I wondered if it was related to knowing about the time she had lost her voice, shortly after starting Little Fish: the months she had been mute, writing songs she couldn't sing, waiting. I wondered if, even now, every time she opened her mouth to exude a note there was an instant – not even a measurable one, just the shadow of something – in which she thought maybe this would be it, nothing would come out, kaput, game over. But then I was taken by the crowd again, by watching their reaction. I knew more or less what I felt – but what would they show?

Great compassion, as it turned out. They smiled when the silence was filled, and smiled even bigger when Juju carried on, sang the rest of the set strongly and loudly. They were part of the story; we were all part of the story, all of us in this strange round building.

After the performance people kept saying – to me, to each other, to Ben and Juju – how good they were, how impressive, how great a performance it had been. It had not been a great performance, I thought – but then again, it had, it had been the greatest of all, in a way.

The truth was I was impressed too; I was impressed to see this manifestation of the close bond between musicians, the support system. But there was something else. It felt like we were all heroes, we were all part of it, part of the small story of tonight, a piece of a larger story. We had helped something happen. We had laughed at all the right places and been uplifted by the redemption. And now we could all celebrate, collectively, our bravery, our victory. But victory over what?

There's a thing about artists, isn't there? The myth, the greatest myth of them all, maybe, is that it's hard to be happy and to create at the same time: the suffering artist, the hungry artist, is the best artist. But what happens if creating something is what makes you happy, or part of what makes you happy? What happens when musicians fall in love – not just with each other, though there is that, but with anyone, anything? What happens when suddenly you're not 18 anymore, banging drums or strumming strings, waiting to either become famous or fall apart?

People go on being musicians, being other things too, even when the romance has worn away, even when they're happy, or approaching happy, even as everything, including their definition of success, is changing. And maybe it's another myth, maybe we really are just a bunch of failures consoling ourselves, licking our wounds: but it seems hard to believe that there isn't a way of making things work, that sometimes going backwards is actually a form of moving forwards, especially when you stop thinking in terms of backwards and forwards and think only in terms of something simpler. Imagine you're young, but not so young anymore that you can't see the possibility of old. Imagine you're in a band, which maybe isn't the band you started out with. And yet here you are: still playing, still evolving, still surviving.

II. Voices

Later, in the upstairs recording room, I noticed something remarkable about Björk's voice. The singers were in a circle, with a microphone positioned in front of each. Björk was usually in the center of the circle or on the outside, with no microphone within reach. Yet whenever she was singing or talking her voice was at the center of the sound. You could pick it out in a second from the Icelandic chatter: the dusky timbre, deep in the mezzo-soprano range; the tremor in it, which occasionally takes on the rasp of a pubescent boy's voice; the way it slices through the sonic haze, as if a few extra frequencies in a given range are being twanged to life. It carries without effort, like those Mongolian voices that can be heard across the steppe. Somehow, the mere fact of her voice became a creative magnet, pulling the music in the right direction.

    — Alex Ross on Björk

I'm not always very good at listening to music.

I listen to it almost constantly – while I'm working, while I'm walking, while I'm on a bus or a train or suspended 30,000 feet above the earth, while I'm evaluating the 200 kinds of peanut butter available for purchase in our local Tesco or staring out the study window watching the leaves fall. But if the word "listen" implies a certain kind of participation, a certain kind of empathy, then I can hardly ever be said to be actually listening to music. I don't even have a set of speakers; sound mainly reaches me through tinny Apple headphones plugged into a phone or a laptop. I rarely sit quietly and focus on music in the same way that I would give a book my full attention. I wonder sometimes about the difference between the way musicians listen to music and the way non-musicians listen to music, and if this inattention of mine is a symptom of my ignorance. I had some very minimal training as a violinist when I was younger, so to the extent that I understand or remember what I learned I can theoretically "deconstruct" a piece of classical music in a way that I simply can't with, say, a Little Fish song. Does this change the way I actually respond to these two different kinds of music? Probably it does. In a sense, it's all about music being contextual – what you hear and how you hear it is influenced not just by emotional or physical circumstances but also by what you know. I know musicians who can tell me exactly what note it is at the end of a song that makes my pulse quicken, but often I hardly hear the notes at all; I certainly don't listen to the lyrics, which interfere with my own thoughts.

It's really only at gigs that I regularly abandon all my anxieties and ambitions, but even then, even then you could say I'm not really listening: I'm just there, along for the ride, trying to use the sounds the performers are making for personal gain, trying to convert their output into a specific and often self-indulgent sensation.

And yet for all my irreverence, my selfishness, music is still a form of escape, a way of subverting the negativity of all those anxieties and ambitions. For this reason, winter is the very best time for music – or perhaps I should say that music is most necessary in winter. When seasonal woe engulfs me, when the world looks overcast and damp and I start to consider the very real possibility that if I remain under this washed-out sky for even a second longer I'll dissolve, become a shadow: there's always a song for that moment.

In fact I tend to go to fewer gigs in the winter, when inertia has set in and to lurch up off my chair and out into the world seems a Herculean task, even though this would be precisely the right time to harness the power of a good loud show. But even in the throes of temporary despair, induced by weak sunlight and heavy rain, I know enough to know to press "play" on whatever device is nearest to me. I don't mean that music is (necessarily) a sort of therapy, a magic amelioration: just that when you're sitting at your desk watching the neighbour's cat climb a naked cherry tree, seeing the frost shimmer on the barren ground, feeling like the blood has frozen in your veins, it is sometimes beneficial to have a human voice in your ear.

❧

It's winter when I meet with Gaz Coombes, lead vocalist and guitarist for Supergrass until the band's split in 2010. On a grey Wednesday morning we sit in his dark studio, drinking dark coffee and discussing music. Down here the world is kept at bay: all the ordinary intrusions are stopped short by staircases, thick doors, the sheer impressiveness of the room, in which he's been writing songs for his new solo album. I'm not sure exactly what sort of quest I'm on, but it seems to me that someone who's been a professional musician his whole working life will almost certainly have some insight into what it means to make music your living. I'm also interested in what it's like to work on a solo project after 17 years as a member of a band – particularly a band like Supergrass, a

band that achieved and maintained objective commercial success. I tell
him that one of the things I'm trying to understand is what happens
when you or your band undergoes a change. I ask him about the solo
album, the motivation behind it.

"I think in a way I sort of felt that I hadn't found my voice," he says.
"We had a collective voice. [...] I'm happy about that. I don't regret
not finding my personal voice earlier on – I think because otherwise
Supergrass wouldn't have been as it was. But it's just a case of like, fuck,
actually man, what would I sound like if I were to do a record, who
would it be?"

Who would it be, indeed? This strikes me as a profound question – as
the question, in a way. Perhaps it's just a slip of the tongue, the accidental
result of speaking quickly and informally, but to ask who would it be,
not what would it be, to imply that the record is animate – not a record
at all, in fact, but a creature or a being in its own right – interests me.
In December I'd heard a live preview of Gaz's new record, and I didn't
know who it was, what it represented: this was not really for me to say.
But I knew I liked it. It had made me tap my toes and feel, for the
duration of the show, quite free, as if suspended in time, briefly and
mercifully unfettered by the shackles of the daily grind. Later, though,
I couldn't remember the music itself in any real detail; I didn't have
any recognizable phrases or melodies in my head, just the memory of
having heard something pleasing. For me music is circumstantial, I remember
writing to a friend once, trying to lay my finger on what, exactly,
happened (or didn't happen) when I listened to music. So I had a
memory of hearing a sound that I had liked but couldn't remember
anymore and I didn't even know if it was the sound or the circumstance
I had enjoyed in the first place: was it just that it was nice to be in a small
warm room hearing noise instead of outside in the pre-Christmas chill,
cold and lonely? I had turned down an opportunity to stand in a chilly
English church and sing carols that evening, I remember: perhaps I was
buzzing because of having asserted myself, because of some small rebellion. But the songs? The songs were incidental. Maybe.

To create a piece of music and to listen to that piece of music: each is,
in its own way, an intensely personal action, a private experience.
Perhaps an album is like a double-sided mirror, showing its creator a
version of himself whilst simultaneously showing the listener some
version of herself. Perhaps, in extreme cases of empathy or ecstasy, there's
some transparency: I can see what he sees and he, maybe, can begin
to see what I see. But while connection between a musician and an

audience member is obviously possible – it happens all the time, in a million different ways – the artist's voice is something that exists independently of that connection; it comes first. If music really is circumstantial, the artist's circumstances matter too.

"In a way, that was my voice at that time," Gaz tells me. "I was interested to see what the concentrated version of myself was."

❦

A voice: a concentrated version of oneself. A wisp of truth, a messenger and a message rolled into one.

One of the first bits of biographical information I ever learned about Little Fish was that for a period immediately after the formation of the band, Juju had lost her voice. A singer unable to sing: I thought of the old adage, the tree falling in the forest. If no one is around to hear it, does it make a sound? She and drummer Nez carried on, writing songs, moving forward even in the soundless abyss, and eventually, with time and work, her voice came back to her.

A year or so ago, I went to talk to Ben and Juju about Little Fish, about their story. They wanted me to write a biography of the band that wasn't just a biography of a band. They wanted something more than a CV, more than just a list of influences. I was a good person to do it, they said, because I didn't know very much about writing band biographies; that is to say, I knew precisely nothing about writing band biographies, because I'd never written one. I did know that most of the ones I'd read started with the phrase "hailing from ..." and followed a fairly predictable pattern.

I didn't know what I was going to write or if it was even a worthwhile exercise; I didn't even trust myself to know enough about music to say what Little Fish sounded like in terms of comparison. I could really only say what they sounded like to me at any given moment. But it was a nice excuse to visit some friends on a hot Sunday afternoon and drink black coffee and eat orange ice lollies and have a chat. I even remember succumbing to a short and foolish fantasy later, about the Rolling Stone reporter 150 years from now who might stumble across my recording of the interview and marvel at this raw, first-hand account of the legendary band's beginnings. I knew it was foolish but I thought it anyway.

In the end I did write the biography, if you can call it that. I tried to piece together the fragments and construct a narrative, but I wasn't sure what shape the narrative should be; this was a band still very much in the midst of things, and it was hard to say with any certainty how to frame it, how to decide where it began and ended. I recorded our conversation on my phone, which I'd placed in the centre of the coffee table. Later I listened back.

"Where do I start from?" Juju says, at the beginning. "Meeting Nez, or before that?"

"Before that," I say, and so we start with Juju, picking up a guitar for the first time at 17 and writing a song. But it could have started any-where: it could have started with Juju's birth, or with her French family, singing songs at the dinner table. It could have started yesterday, or with the dawn of time.

It was funny to write about people I knew, but even funnier to write about them knowing that everything would change, that it had already changed, that there were aspects of the truth not addressed, either as a result of omission or ignorance: there were things I could never know, things you will never know, things even the band didn't really know. The finished product was a story about adding and subtracting, really. It was a very human story – the only human story, in a sense, the one about surviving, adapting to your surroundings. And the thing is, of course, it wasn't a finished product, it is never a finished product: a band is not frozen in time, their music is not static. Only a few months later I was revising what I'd written to account for the departure of Nez. And I could keep making changes, at regular intervals, probably indefinitely, but I don't: at a certain point I think whatever you say or write about a band becomes part of their past; nothing can stay current forever.

One day Ben sent me an email containing some digital photographs of an old Velvet Underground album he'd picked up in London. "Best liner notes ever?" was the subject of the email, and as I opened the files, I realized that the photographs were of an essay by Elliot Murphy.

"I wish I was writing this a hundred years from today," Murphy opens his essay. "Then, I'd be writing about music made by dead people. There'd be a beginning and an end."

It's easy to write about music made by dead people, or it seems easy, anyway. The reason it seems easy is not because they're dead, but because once they're dead they can't keep changing, though our percep-tion of them might. Trying to write a sentence about a band that's very much alive and kicking, let alone a book about them, is a crazy idea, because just when you think you've started to understand who they are and what they do, something's shifted.

A few days after I read Elliot Murphy's liner notes, though, I came across music critic Alex Ross's Listen to This, a book of essays about everyone from Mozart to Radiohead. "The difficult thing about music writing, in the end, is not to describe a sound but to describe a human being," Ross writes. "It's tricky work, presumptuous in the case of the living and speculative in the case of the dead." So perhaps Murphy was wrong: even the dead are not done changing, not done saying new things. There is no beginning and no end; just what we choose to extrapolate from our own encounters with a sound or a song.

There are, of course, musicians that have sounded pretty much the same throughout their careers. I think of a video interview that Juju did with Debbie Harry as part of a project on women in rock; when asked, "Were you ever told to change or maintain your image by the record company at the height of Blondie's success?" Harry responds: "No, but I think record companies, once they have decided on a marketing strategy, and have any kind of success with their marketing strategy, they don't want you to change. They don't want you to grow as an artist, or, you know, do anything different [...] I wasn't dead set on anything ... I was experimenting and finding my way through different ideas."

Veterans of the industry know this happens, and so do listeners. When I first started talking to people about this idea, a number of them, without prompting, cited Coldplay as an example of a band who'd found something that made money and stuck with it: a band who essentially recorded the same song over and over again. This was not necessarily a judgement of worth, just an observation, one with which you might disagree; you might say, "look, no, this album may sound like it sounds like that album, but the groove is totally different, man, it's a totally different sound even if it sounds like it sounds the same." One of the things I'm learning is that there isn't very much that's safe to say about music. But here's what I do think is safe to say: Little Fish isn't one of those bands that has sounded pretty much the same throughout their career. Most bands are probably not one of those bands.

Which seems about right, to me. We talk about voice, about finding your voice, and indeed losing your voice: but the search for "a concentrated version of myself" is an ongoing process. Maybe it's never-ending. What if you find your voice for one album, and discover it's different for the next? What if you wake up ten years into your career and understand, finally, that what you've been doing is not an accurate representation of who you are? It happens in life as in music, after all.

So there's something unnatural about things that are too fixed. Because of the way circumstances change, because of the way your life is not the same as it was a year ago, no matter what's happened or not happened, it feels right that a band won't write the same album twice; it feels right that they may sound completely different. You may identify the timbre of a familiar singing voice but recognize nothing else about the music itself. This is disappointing, sometimes, as a fan; when you pinpoint what it is you like, what it is that makes you feel the way you want to feel, then that's often all you want, you want to drown yourself in that sound. I do this on a daily basis, finding the song that makes me feel just right enough to do whatever it is I need to do that day, pressing repeat, and repeat again, and repeat again, trying to hold on to the feeling for as long as possible.

But what speaks to listeners isn't always a specific sound. Music is not always a drug, something we do to feel a certain way. Often there's something else, something bigger, that compels us to follow a band from one album to the next, to support them in every incarnation. As one Little Fish fan tweeted after the band announced some upcoming changes: "For me @Littlefishmusic is more than just music, it represents freedom of expression and honesty, which is rare!" [1]

I've heard a number of different Little Fish sounds. The first time I heard them play live they were nervous because the venue was much smaller than they'd imagined and they worried the pound of the drums and the roar of Juju's voice would overpower the room (it didn't). I've seen Juju, accompanied by just a piano, perform the slow, comparatively mellow *Heroin Dance*; she curled up on a chair, no microphone, rocking back and forth to the notes. To a crowd of thousands at the Westonbirt Arboretum the band was big, loud; at a local open mic night a few weeks later, Ben played harmonica and Juju played foot-tapping acoustic guitar.

Some of this is situational, of course, a demonstration of musical versatility; but there's also a kind of inevitability to it. I often think that there's no such thing as "adulthood", that the process of growing up happens and continues to happen until the moment we die, even if we die in extreme old age, centurions with great-grandchildren. In the same way, I wonder if there's no such thing as a definitive sense of artistic self, if one's character is never quite solidified, if we might be crazy to expect some great moment of clarity, some ultimate, final version of ourselves.

The pressures on musicians are heavy and various, and sooner or later any conversation about "voice" arrives at the tension between "commercialism" — *will anybody want to hear this?, will it sell?*, and "authenticity" — *is this saying what I want it to say? Is this me?*

One afternoon I meet with Theo Whitworth, who plays guitar for Spring Offensive, a young Oxford-based five-piece band. I've heard Spring Offensive play live a few times. Since I began this book and started talking seriously with Ben and Juju and others about the business of music, I've tried to avoid saying things like "they're going to be huge someday!" I know how meaningless it is to say that — about a band, an author, anyone. What is huge? And how could you possibly predict, whether you're a punter or an industry professional, the trajectory that any artist's career will take? But my instinct, the first time I heard Spring Offensive play (acoustic, overflowing on a tiny stage) was to want to tell people that they were a band who "are really going to go somewhere!" I've refrained from saying it out loud to anyone, for fear of being thought naïve, but continued to think it, in spite of myself, in spite of all that I know and don't know about what it means to be in a band. The difference between acoustic Spring Offensive and plugged-in Spring Offensive is marked, and I strongly prefer their acoustic sound — but maybe that's more to do with intimacy than music, more to do with the way you feel you're a part of something when you're in a cramped dark space inches away from the performers. Maybe when I heard them play for the first time and thought, "they're going to go somewhere!" it was because I wanted to be part of that momentum, and it was possible to imagine how I could be, if we never left this room: the audience, the band, the venue itself, were all an integral part of some forward motion.*

It occurs to me that voice is dependent upon your specific idea of success. When I ask Theo about this, about what success would mean to him, he tells me, echoing Leonard Cohen,[2] that "success is survival" — being able to do this full-time, for all five members of the band to quit their day jobs and focus on the music. But, he adds, it has to be on your own terms. He says they're aware of what has commercial appeal and what doesn't, but they don't write and perform songs with commerciality explicitly in mind — the band is still theirs, the sound still belongs to them, and so, in a sense, does their future.

---

* In July 2012 Spring Offensive's single *Worry Fill My Heart* was added to the BBC Radio 1 playlist — a major boon for a band hoping to break out of the ranks of the unheard-of.

Other musicians seem to see the distinction between artistry and commercialism as more clear-cut, the line between them less forgiving. In another interview with Juju about women in rock, singer and song-writer Carina Round says, "There's two different sides to the industry. There's the art side, in my opinion, and the money side, and of course they cross over sometimes, but I think one or the other is more preva-lent, and if you're getting into the industry for the money, then, you know, do what you gotta do for the money, and don't be heartbroken when your art gets taken away. And if you're getting into it for artistic reasons, do what you've gotta do for the art, and don't be surprised if you're doing it poor, or less comfortably than you sometimes would like to be living."

In the same series of interviews, Sierra Swan says:

> The question is what success is to an individual. Is success, you know, *American Idol*, and making tons of money? Or is success doing truly what you want, and following through with your instincts 100%, and not changing anything for anybody? You know, for me that's success now. I do what I want.

It's possible, of course, that making tons of money and doing what you want are not incompatible – even in music. It's certainly possible that the whole thing is vastly more complicated than the black and white world in which you either suffer for your art or sell out. In his ebook *Music in the Digital Age*, academic and author Andrew Dubber, who lectures in music industries innovation at Birmingham City University, writes that, "There's this widely held idea that music is this pure and natural expression that happens creatively and artistically among human beings, and then commerce comes along and corrupts it all. I say that's obvious nonsense. Music and Commerce aren't individual concepts or entities that exist "over there", separate from People. Music and Commerce are both Things That People Do." Humans are the connecting force, and voice is human. The tension between authenticity and commercialism need not define your voice, because your voice is not necessarily dependent on your idea of success. Your idea of success might well influence your voice, but definitions of success change too, remember. Everything changes, keeps changing. What once seemed like a "pure and natural expression" may now seem like a lie; what once seemed like the path to obscurity may now seem like the path to fulfillment; what once seemed hollow may now seem right. In a sense, voice transcends "selling out", transcends the "industry", transcends even "art": it's the one thing that carries us from one moment to the next, the only essential thing.

❦

As my interview with Gaz comes to a close, I can't resist asking him about his perception of the changes in Little Fish's music. I tell him I wonder what audiences feel. The fans I know and have spoken to are invariably and tirelessly supportive, but a cynical part of me wonders if there aren't people out there sitting around thinking, *this isn't what I signed up for; I wanted Juju screaming into a microphone, pouring water over her fans, kicking amps, not this tame little ukulele song, not this new thing, this new line-up, this unfamiliar territory*.

"I would imagine Little Fish fans, if they're like me, and I'm a fan, would just be like, 'come on, just hit me with it, throw it at me, I'm waiting to hear what you do next, I know that as long as you're singing, it's gonna be great'," he tells me. "You know, for me, it's all just about her [Juju's] voice. She's an incredible character, great personality, great on stage, and she's got this amazing voice. I don't give a shit if she's scream-ing or like, singing as soft as, like, a whispering vocal – it's Juju's voice, and it's amazing either way."

I nod my agreement. It's about the voice, her voice, more than anything else; and whatever that voice is doing is going to be interesting to the people who have – for whatever reason, for any reason – connected with it.

What, then, are we actually attaching ourselves to when we listen to a band and decide we like them? The answer, if my conversations with Gaz and with Little Fish are any indicator, is that, while it may vary, it's probably the artist, the person who resides in the music – even if we know close to nothing about who that person is except what we can intuit from the particular quality of their voice or the way they press the keys on the piano.

Discussing the newest Little Fish line-up, which includes a new drum-mer and a second vocalist, Ben tells me that he thinks it looks like the inside of Juju's head; it feels like a visual representation of what goes on when she thinks and writes and sings. Maybe it will all be different in a few years: I don't know, it's possible even they don't know, not for sure. "The artist that you truly are inside" is no more set in stone than the length of your hair or the kind of guitar you play need be; there are internal doubts and hopes to account for, external pressures and influences. There are all the things that might happen to make you different from the way you were. And yet somewhere there is a constant – some kernel of selfhood, some tone or colour that feels true. And maybe that's what we mean when we talk about voice: truth, even if it's just truth in a single, independent moment.

This is the biography I wrote for Little Fish; it gives a potted history, but really it tries to capture where they were in 2011, a sort of in-between time, after the release of their debut album but before the formation of a new line-up in March 2012.

The evolution of Little Fish

First there was Juju, who picked up a guitar for the first time at 17 and wrote a song. She went on writing songs. Eventually she wrote a song called Little Fish and played it in a pub. No one at the pub knew her name, but they knew that song, and she saw one day as she walked past that she had been billed on the sign outside as Little Fish.

So then there was a name, although of course it was a name for something that hadn't happened yet. There was just a possibility, underpinning everything.

Then there was a strange dark period in Juju's life. She fell under spells and then simply fell ill, like her body was rejecting a poison, saying, "you're in the wrong place, Juju, get out."

So she got out. She met Nez in a chip shop. He was a drummer, though he hadn't been drumming for a while. Juju had lost her voice, but they started a band anyway and called it Little Fish. And so instead of being the end – this unlikely alliance of two unlikely people, the drummer who hadn't been drumming much lately, the singer whose voice had been lost in a sea of confusion – it was the beginning, or at least, another beginning.

They played in the garage. Juju kept writing songs that she couldn't sing and saying everything would be okay next week and it never was. Until eventually, one day, it was. After many, many hours working alone in a rehearsal room and some sessions in Alexander Technique, Juju found her voice again.

She and Nez did a demo and got some gigs. And for two years they did gig after gig after gig, driving up and down the country, making a name for themselves, gathering fans, gaining momentum.

One day Linda Perry heard their music and flew to Oxford to hear them play. The thing about hearing Little Fish play is that it's like the slap in the face you need to wake up, the sweet kiss at night: people hear Little Fish play live and their breath is torn away from them and then restored, and things change. So they were signed to Custard Records and recorded their debut album *Baffled and Beat* in Los Angeles.

Then Little Fish added a layer and became a three-piece. They had put Hammond on *Baffled and Beat* and wanted a Hammond player in the band, and along came Ben. Juju met him at a rehearsal in Oxford; he was playing the piano and when he was done the first thing she asked him was if he played the Hammond – then she made small talk, asked his name, but her focus had always been the songs, the band, and this focus, this myopic drive, had always been the thing that carried them forward.

Ben did, as it turns out, play the Hammond. Like Nez he was a trained musician, a perfect complement to self-taught Juju, with her irresistible irreverence for musical rules and regulations.

This marked another kind of beginning. Little Fish left Custard to pursue an independent career. They did the opposite of what every rock star narrative says you should do: they came home again. This is important; the fierce sense of community, of origin and independence, matters to the songs that Little Fish write and play. The rock'n'roll myth was still just a myth: being signed, being discovered, had not brought Little Fish fortune, but they still knew why

they made music and they still knew they had to make
music, somehow, anyhow.

But independence, even when you've chosen it, can be
hard. There was still the rent to pay; there were still bills
and struggles. Now Nez had a family, and a decision to
make, because life is not always kind, and sometimes one
thing you love needs you more than the other thing you
love. Sometimes it is simply not possible to devote yourself
wholly to music and also, at the same time, to support
yourself, your children.

So they were a two-piece again, like they had been in the
beginning. Their sound changed a little to accommodate
the departure of their beloved drummer, but their spirit
did not. And the truth, the heart of the matter, is this:
Little Fish is a band that gets closer to the fans, the root of
the story and of the song, with every moment that passes
and everything that happens to them. They have toured
with Supergrass, Spinnerette, Juliette Lewis, Alice in Chains,
Placebo; Debbie Harry saw them supporting Courtney Love
and asked them to join Blondie for a UK tour. But still they
remain steady, devoted to their roots. The music has not had
its soul polished away; it's not electronic, vapid, perfect. It's
also not provincial; Little Fish are local on an emotional
rather than a political level. Everything happens in a small
space, but nothing is small. They're as comfortable playing
house parties as they are the Royal Albert Hall. Almost
everyone they work with nowadays is Oxford-based –
producers, photographers, artists – but this is not snobbery
or small-mindedness, it's organic, it's part of the band's
narrative.

They do things differently: their sound, their ethos, is
eclectic, and they aren't afraid of collaboration or experi-
mentation. Through it all, they've been close with their
fans, and their fans – these rabid, beautiful fans, each of
whom seems to find some unique meaning in the arc of a
song or the depth of Juju's voice – have always been close
with them, too. The relationship is reciprocal, and perhaps
this is the final stage of the evolution. Little Fish started as
one woman, and became a feeling, a momentum. They say

they don't always know where they're going, but they're definitely going somewhere, with a whole community in tow.

This is an update that Juju wrote in February 2012 to let Little Fish fans know about some upcoming changes and, perhaps more importantly, the history behind those changes. It's a good example of the kind of honesty that the band has often been lauded for — and of the kinds of challenges and changes that bands encounter on their journey towards discovering a comfortable voice.

Little Fish 2012 Update

I never quite know what I'm going to write before I start writing.

It's just the way that writing has always happened to me. I woke up this morning with a feeling that I should write something to you to explain a little about what has been going on in Fishville, behind the scenes, within our Rubik's Cube, in my head.

Second album?

At the end of 2010, I promised you all a second album. The catalyst for this was Linda. Little Fish was on Linda's record label Custard/Universal at the time. Linda wanted us to make a second record and we were to have it finished and delivered to her in the space of about ten days. The urgency for this was based on the promise of a tour around America with her new band Deep Dark Robot. For as much of a shock as this was to the system, Nez and I were prepared to take on the challenge. Nez and I were always prepared to dig deep and do the work necessary for the band to survive.

We always thought that *Baffled & Beat* maybe hadn't had the rawness that people had expected of us, and so were thrilled to have a chance to correct this with another album. Unfortunately, after an initial burst of energy to get things rolling we received legal demands from the label that were very different to the ones we remembered from our initial signing. For us to make the record we would have had to comply with Linda's demand. Had we signed, Nez and I would have been signed into the label for many years with no guarantee of ever making any money from any of the record sales or even having a budget to tour. It made no sense for us to make this record. We couldn't afford to continue to live without making any money. Nez already had a child and supporting his family was of primary importance. This wasn't a time for risk taking.

As a consequence, we asked to leave the label. We were lucky that we could do this and that they let us go. They could no longer fulfill their part of the contract for financial reasons of their own, and we were able to leave the deal without any ill feelings. So at the start of 2011, although Little Fish was without a label and pretty skint, we were free to do our own thing. Neither Nez or myself have seen any money from any of the record sales of *Baffled & Beat*. I am not saying that we are owed any money as I know that the label has to recoup what you sign for before this ever happens, but nobody has ever showed us any accounting. Who knows? All I know is that Universal/Island (our UK label) sold all the copies they printed and nobody ever sent us anything.

Rocker
Being signed to a major record label was an experience. Some of it was great and for a lot of it, I will always be grateful. We got to travel a lot, meet great people, do some great tours and have a lot of fun. Before going to LA I had only ever really travelled to my French grandparents' summer house in the middle of the French mountains.

One thing, however, that I found hurtful and harmful in the whole process was losing a sense of myself. I lost the sense of who I was, why I was writing songs and the direction I wanted my life to go. To be part of Little Fish, I had to lose part of myself, give part of myself, lose my whole. To be in a band is to be in a democracy. Nez and myself were both democrats. Being a slight conflict avoider, I now realize that I agreed and did a lot of things that actually I didn't want to do and should never have done. I should have done far more research before I signed my record deal, and maybe even understood who I was before I let things sweep me away.

I think I slipped into the role of "rocker". I understand why this was. I see that I can be slightly insane on stage, that I can sing loudly and not be the most compliant stereotype when it comes to being a woman. I suppose a part of this was my decision, as I have never wanted to be seen as a singer-songwriter. For me, music has always been a "team sport". Something that you do with other people to share with other people. I wanted to be part of a gang. I wanted to be heard.

I don't like the stereotype of the typical female singer-songwriter. I would hate nothing more than to be alone and travelling. I always wanted to experience music and happenings with other people. So, yes, becoming a rocker was my doing.

Having said all this, I need to make another thing clear. There is another side to the story, to the bullet. I was also in a band with a great drummer who I suppose was a rocker. When we started the band, I was young and didn't have the knowledge or experience that I now have. I tried to present all sorts of alternative songs and quirks to Little Fish, but I suppose they just never stuck with Nez. As I said, being in band is a democracy (well for me it has been) and I wanted Nez to be happy and play things he enjoyed. This was important to me. He was important to me. The alternative suggestions always got vetoed. Nobody really ever went for them. Not Nez and not Linda. So, becoming the stereotype of "the rock chick" was kind of inevitable. It wasn't thought out. Being a rocker was never all that I was and never all that I wanted to be.

It has taken me a year now to understand all this. Last year, I wrote another album. It wasn't as rocky as the first. My manager liked the songs but kept telling me that there was no "hit" song. We had no funding. Nez left. Things kind of fell apart. There I was. No drummer. No way of getting my songs recorded. I was stuck I suppose. I didn't admit it at the time because I don't like quitting and I don't like giving up. I felt very lost.

After Nez left, we released *Wonderful* simply because it was ready to go. Had there been an album to follow, it would have been the first single from it. Although the album has been demoed, it will only ever exist in the lost files on my computer. I doubt anything will ever come of it.

Dead year

This takes us to October 2011. Nothing happened for Little Fish last year. It was what I call a "dead" year. These years happen. They aren't particularly pleasant and I wouldn't wish them on anybody. I was starting to get depressed and wonder if I should just forget music and start a new career. I had no idea what but I knew that if I had to, then I would. After the kickbacks, I was feeling defeated. The record deal was never the deal I thought it would be in terms of "how it is to be signed to a label". Everything had been tough. Dealing with lawyers, ex-managers, record companies, people, opinions, criticized. All of this happening because one day, I had sat at my desk and started to write songs. I felt like I had gotten nowhere after all the years of hard work and sacrifice. I wasn't happy. All this was never what I had signed up for.

I suppose I didn't write a song after this for about four months, which for me was an eternity. I felt that I had nothing to say and no reason to say it. I knew that there were many other musicians out there with far more hunger and focus and desire to succeed. I didn't feel I could ever have the energy to go through it all again. I started sleeping.

DIY

Today, I couldn't be feeling happier or better. Something in me has changed. I have understood something crucial. I have stopped weeping and moaning about the past and blaming and living behind myself. I took the decision last month, when I could see myself becoming someone that I didn't want to become and wouldn't want to be around, that I was to only look forward and live in the present. To stop the "what ifs" and "if onlys". I haven't looked back. Ben and I have done up an old garage and with the bits of gear that we have, we started recording. A month or so ago, Ben pushed me to record a Beatles cover, and it seems to have catalysed something in me to want to sing and play music again. I feel like I have rediscovered myself and found the direction that I want to go in and also possibly, the direction that I have always wanted to go in. I love quirky songs and quirky music and quirky instrumentation. That has always been me, but I haven't ever been able to show this side to people. I was stuck as the "female rocker from Little Fish".

This last month, I have been writing a whole new sound and a whole new set of songs. I have decided that I don't want to go deaf and be shouting over loud drums, I want to simply be able to sing. I want to put the colour into the songs that I have never been able or allowed to do. We were a two-piece and Nez wasn't the best singer, so harmonies were always out of the question. I can sing in French. I can do what I like and nobody can stop me. We have our own little recording set up. I don't have to rely on anybody else. I can record one drum at a time and then another and make my own drum loop or pattern. I have also stopped sending any of the music that I have been recording to our management. I don't need negative feedback about "hits". People thought that *Darling Dear* or *Am I Crazy* would be hits. And they weren't. We could hardly even get any radio play. So, why should I care about this "hit"? What do other people really know?

I always wrote music because it was something that I did. I never did it to be famous. I wrote music and sang because it was fun and I felt like I could express myself. One day I realized that if I had a little bit of success, then it might be possible for me to travel and see the world and be happy doing something that I loved. I feel like I have found this person again. The person who first started writing songs all those years ago. I am not joining in with the "write a hit" thing, the pressure that the industry so pushed on me. It squeezed every bit of creativity out of me. Feeling free is a much better feeling.

And so, I have put a new band together. The line-up is different to Little Fish's old incarnation. I'm not going to explain that all now. I will let you discover it for yourself. But I just wanted to let you know, that nothing that I am doing now is random, it is something that I really want to do. It is very different to any Little Fish music you will have heard before. Part of me realizes that you might not like it and that is fair enough, but this music is my choice and for now it makes me very happy.

Big news

Thank you for reading this blog update. I never intended on writing it all up this way but I realized when I started that in order for you to understand the present, you would have to understand the past. And if you have got this far with us on this journey you deserve to be told, by me, that I am expecting a child. I am to become a parent in July.

So the new record will be recorded by July, but only released in early 2013. We will be doing a few shows before then, but afterwards have a break while I learn to live with my child and become a mother. I will be able to do this with peace and tranquility, knowing that I have achieved something for myself beforehand. I also want to get this record done so that I don't have the stresses of "I need to write a record" lurking constantly around my mind. The record will be ready and you may well see little videos popping up on YouTube in the lead-up.

Big love to you.
JuJu XX

III. Relationships

At 14 I fell in love for the first time. He was in a band and we shared a passion for music, or perhaps I should say we shared a prejudice about music: we each considered our tastes to be vastly superior to those of pretty much anyone else, at least in our age group, and we both believed firmly that you could judge a person by what was in her portable CD player. He was the only boy who had ever shown me any positive attention, and we spent three blissful months making out in the library during lunch before, just as school was letting out for the summer, he dumped me. At the time it was unexpected, though in retrospect the line "I've told other girls I loved them, but this time I really mean it" delivered two weeks into our relationship as earnestly as a slightly spotty and very scrawny high school freshman in a Blink-182 t-shirt could possibly deliver it, should have been a clue that this was more a spring-time fling than a great love affair.

I duly spent the summer sulking – about the break-up, initially, but then about everything, anything. My best friend and I adopted a uniform that I hoped conveyed our adolescent outrage at the unfairness of love and life; we dyed our hair, painted our fingernails black, ripped our fishnet stockings, wore shirts that were deliberately (and not at all flat-teringly) too small, bought plastic studded belts and slung them around our tiny waists like a beauty queen's sash. I played a song called *Why Doesn't Anybody Like Me?* by a band called No Use For a Name on repeat. (When I listen to this song now, for research purposes, I can't tell if I'm uncomfortable because it reminds me so powerfully of my own teenage awkwardness or because it's simply very bad music.)

And we went to gigs, dropped off and then picked up a few hours later by our baffled parents. Each time I heard an angry lyric I imagined that it was an expression of my own sentiments; I liked to think that every song had been written for me, to use against whomever or whatever had scorned me. Music, I had discovered, is not just about what you hear; it's also about what you feel.

At home I listened to women, too, but when we went to live acts it was always to see men, pale-faced sweaty men who jackhammered their way through each song. I suppose I had it in my head that there was something inherently sexual about live music, that it was a situation in which fantasy became acceptable (I thought it was tacky to imagine a film star might sweep me off my feet, but it was not outside the realm of possibility that some bassist or other might catch my eye as I bounced enthusiastically at the front of a small crowd). Some of them were real heart-throbs, or so we thought; we were bored of the clean-faced, drug-addled boys of our private school, their popped collars and Abercrombie & Fitch tracksuit bottoms. We liked the swollen piercings of our pop-punk idols, the greasy hair and thin limbs, the idea that not every male specimen was a pot-smoking lacrosse star with an expensive car and a difficult relationship with his parents. We stood as close to the stage as we dared, while beer-soaked undergraduates from the local university jumped up and down on our Converse-clad feet. I did sometimes sense that there was something desperate about this, that our reaction to these performances we viewed and revered was somehow sterile, predictable, temporary. One of the songs we liked began with a short exchange between a stern sounding couple, who describe their child as being in the *punk phase*. For a while it had seemed a perfect expression of how little the adults, or even most of our peers, could possibly understand – of course other people thought it was just a *phase*, but I knew better, this was deeper than that, would last longer, maybe even forever. At the same time, I knew it wasn't, and wouldn't, like I knew when my first boyfriend said he loved me that it was a different kind of love, but went on to be disappointed anyway.

As summer ended I found that the thing which had initially given me comfort had become something that felt safe, and one thing I knew was that music should not feel safe. It didn't always need to rile or challenge – I knew that, I knew it could comfort or soothe – but it should do *something*, and I had started to feel nothing at all when I heard the man

place air quotes around "the punk phase", followed by the first predictable rhythms of the song. So I dyed my hair back (our school had a rule
about hair, anyway – it had to be a natural colour, and I was pretty sure
that Merlot was considered natural amongst vintners but not hairdress-
ers or school authorities). Our school had a rule about shirts, too: they
had to be long enough to cover your entire torso. My appearance
regressed but I had moved forwards, moved on. I didn't want a steady
beat and a scrawny twenty-something boy whining about the hot girl
who had snubbed him. I wanted a different rhythm and a different song.

It's a complicated business, having a relationship with music, and anybody who listens to music has a relationship with it, if even just for a few
minutes. There are so many ways to relate to it: as a fan, as a musician,
as an industry professional. And yet the thing itself, the music, remains
tantalizingly intangible, a kind of chameleon, taking on the colour of
the room you're in when you hear it or the songwriter's mood as he
crafts the lyrics. "All I've got to put in a song is my own experience,"
Leonard Cohen tells Dorian Lynskey in an interview for the *Guardian*.[3] But
you could invert the sentiment, too: *all I've got to get out of a song is my own
experience.*

I remember my mother driving me to school when I was about ten
years old; she had a tape with four different versions of Cohen's *Famous
Blue Raincoat* on it, which we listened to often. What did I know about the
complications of adult love (or even cold winters, for that matter – I'd
only ever lived in sunny southern California)? But when I heard the
song, sung by Cohen himself in his drowsy way or Joan Baez with her
clear rich voice, I had an image in my head, nevertheless, of shadows, an
obscured figure in a blue Burberry (a lucky guess), a frosted window. It
cooled the hot California afternoons, or gave me hope, in the mornings,
that the world was more mysterious than I knew, bigger than this empty
stretch of highway and the bullies and bores at school. And while I've
written about the two-sided mirror, the separation between artist and
listener, there is also an undeniable interface; ultimately the relationship
– however strong or weak it may be, whatever the impact it may have on
writing or listening to music – is at the centre of a song.

"This is a conversation," writes Andrew Dubber, whose work as an academic, author and consultant revolves around radio and music:

> It's human beings, communicating with each other. That's it. The whole message in a nutshell: This is a conversation. And by "this", I mean the whole thing – the music, the medium, the marketing, the technology, the relationship with fans, the branding, the community music workshops, the recordings, the live concerts, the social media profile pages, the improvisations, the downloads, the t-shirts, the BitTorrents, the ringtones, the status updates, the copyright laws, the CDs, the vinyl, the day to day work of being a musician, the inspired musical expression.

Everything, in other words, is about relationships. Nothing is isolated. When we talk about music we don't talk just about notes on a page, sounds coming through speakers, A&R men "discovering talent", bands standing on a stage. We talk about how this song relates to us, or how that album relates to a particular period in an artist's history, or how the band relates to its influences and predecessors. We talk about points of convergence: we talk about where the perception of the artist and the perception of the listener meet. When we say music, or when I say music, at least, this is what I mean: the thing that encapsulates all these relationships and experiences, the thing that needs to be made, heard, and felt in order to really exist.

In a 2004 profile of Björk, Alex Ross describes a conversation with the musician, pointing out that, "Björk often uses the second person to close the distance between herself and others." At its best, music does this too, organically: sound and memory erase distance, so that when you listen to a song, there's very little standing between you and the person who wrote it, the person who's performing it. On the other hand, there's everything standing between the two of you: the sum of all of the things you know and all of the things she knows, all of the things neither of you can ever know. The overlap and the chasm are the same thing, come from the same place. "It's human beings, communicating with each other."

The thing I noticed right away about Little Fish, apart from Juju's notoriously sonorous voice, was the relationship they had with their fans. The "Squids", as the band calls their most devoted followers, seemed to be an integral part of the whole operation. There was no distance between the band and the audience: when you saw them live you always sensed that some of Juju's Hulk-like energy was sourced directly from the corresponding energy of reverent listeners, that there was some kind of alchemy or sorcery going on. I remember going to see Juju, quite soon after I first met her, do a solo acoustic set in Oxford. For the last song Ben joined her on the piano, and Juju curled up in a chair and sang Heroin Dance with such quiet intensity that it seemed impossible to imagine that she was just another human being, like you or me: she couldn't have the same banal conversations, you thought, or spill a drink, or run for a bus, or miss an appointment. She was elsewhere, other-worldly. And then we went to a pub next door and she sat with friends and fans (friends who were also fans, fans who were also friends) and it was as if she had never been that wracked creature on stage; just another girl, at the pub in the evening.

Like most bands, Little Fish depend in various ways on their supporters – the fans who will trek miles to see them play on even the smallest stage, who will shell out money for merchandise and music, who will spread the word, are crucial to the band's continued existence. But you always get the sense that there is something reciprocal about this; the Little Fish fans I've met and spoken with lead me to think that the band has consistently been engaging and respectful. "I'm always really surprised that we have fans," Juju tells me. "I'm always really appreciative. I think because it was such hard work to even get anywhere, I've always appreciated any support. And I just think it's human decency to appreciate people, and to care about them. They care about us, I care about them. I really do."

One Saturday afternoon I meet Ben and Juju for lunch; their friend and fan Sophie is visiting from Manchester, and I'm keen to speak to a Squid who isn't Oxford-based, since there are so many dotted across the globe who I've never met in person. I ask Sophie about how it feels when a band you follow and love begins to change. "In that situation," Sophie tells me, "the relationship with the fans is more important." She speaks about being drawn to a band "as people, rather than just the music". It's hard to listen selfishly to music: you get swept up by the narrative of the people making it, becomes a part of your own.

"The diehard fans will always like whatever you do," Sophie adds. "It's just the others, the people who only buy a few albums a year, that might decide not to buy yours if it's not quite the same as the last one, I guess." She says it seems to her that Little Fish have more diehard fans, proportionally, than many other bands do. I don't know how to measure this, I don't know if it's statistically accurate, but the sentiment rings true: it's the thing I first felt about them, the thing I've continued to feel, as I follow them on their meandering journey. Perhaps every band needs to believe that this is the case, for them, that they attract a uniquely loyal group of devotees. But it strikes me that Little Fish really are good at forging strong bonds.

I remember attending a house concert once; a small group, maybe 20 or 30 people, gathered in someone's sprawling Victorian home, crowded into a room downstairs to hear a singer-songwriter perform some of his music. After the performance, I stood in the kitchen with the singer-songwriter's girlfriend, chatting, sipping wine.

"It's a gift, this evening," she told me. "We should be grateful. He's given us a gift. He doesn't have to share his music with us like this."

Well, yes, I thought: in some sense this was true. He was an excellent musician, the performance had been intimate and weirdly moving (although maybe that was partly the wine), and although people sometimes speak of the compulsion to create, the almost obsessive drive to write a novel or an album, he was not bound to share his creations with anyone, certainly not us. But I worried about the arrogance of suggesting that gratitude was obligatory, or that somehow the audience was just a bunch of hungry young birds, mouths open to passively receive and internalize the offering, offering nothing in return. Even now I find it hard to pinpoint what grated me about the girlfriend's suggestion – perhaps it was the way it was delivered, as if I needed reminding that I had just seen something good, or perhaps it was the late hour, the fact that I was getting over a particularly nasty cold, something that had nothing to do with her and certainly nothing to do with the man who had just strummed his guitar and sung for an audience of mainly strangers. But I worried about the distance we create between ourselves and the artists whose work we admire, or the distance that's created by others: I worried that maybe, when we did this, we were missing something.

And yet I know, logically, that distance from an artist is not always a bad thing. Quite the contrary. I think of the boys my friend and I watched during the summer following my first pathetic heartbreak – would I have wanted to meet them? Almost certainly not, even if I didn't know it at the time; I was too busy projecting my own hopes and anxieties onto them; there was no room for any actual interaction, no room for a real life relationship, however inconsequential, and anyway it would have spoiled the fun of imagining. I'm not alone in this; Sophie, for instance, tells me about the time an uncle offered to arrange for her to meet Sharleen Spiteri from Texas. "I couldn't do it," Sophie says. "She was like my ultimate idol, but I think even if I met her now, or if she was on Twitter, I don't think I could follow her. You know? What if she said something really stupid?"

"You don't want to destroy an image," I suggest. There's an aspect of being a performer that's not just being yourself, but being somebody that people will look at and, often, up to. It's a fragile relationship, for a fan as much as for an artist: balancing what you need to get out of the other person, whether that's private or overt (a fan might simply need some comfort which the sound of her favourite singer's voice affords, a singer might need a fan to buy a t-shirt) with who that other person is. As a fan, you're having to match what you want from an artist with who that artist is at her core. Sometimes those things are compatible – sometimes you can be best friends with a singer you also admire deeply on an artistic level – but other times you need to maintain a certain distance; you need to believe your own stories about the person in order to get what it is you feel their music can give you.

Perhaps, for Little Fish, it's that part of their essence is the community around them, the community they're part of, the community they've helped create. No matter how many iterations of Little Fish there end up being, it's Juju's voice and that community that keep the heart of the band beating. Distance, here, does no one any good: their music relies on an interaction, a human touch.

❧

There's a slightly less savoury side to this, of course. Fans are, theoretically, how a band makes money, gets famous. Without fans – punters, really – you can have no record sales, no platinum albums, no mansions, no food on the table at all, unless you supplement your income with something else, as so many musicians must. The line between playing as a hobby and playing for a living is a thin one indeed, and it's almost invisible until you find yourself slipping across it: one minute you're pounding your drums or singing your songs for a roomful of people, and the next you realize you've got to get back to reality, got to address, one way or another, the pile of bills and succumb to the pull of other obligations. Music may be a conversation, but it's also an industry, a business, a world in which everyone is trying to sell you something all the time – an album, an idea, a t-shirt, a persona, a dream, a future, a past, a tote bag. Some of these things cost money; others cost dignity, or time. But in every case there's room for cynicism; there's a relationship to develop with the beast itself, with the necessity of making a living, the necessity of fitting in somewhere.

In *The Answer Is The Ecosystem: Marketing Music Through Non-Linear Communication*, a 2011 thesis, communication consultant Bas Grasmayer poses the question, "how can 2AM [a record label] effectively market their music to fans by using the web?"[4] The answer he proposes, you probably won't be surprised to learn, is "the ecosystem" ("an active fan base which is interconnected through non-linear communication"). Grasmayer outlines a set of steps to success. In the first step, "a band, group, artist, label, has to differentiate themselves [...] their music has to be very good, but it also needs an element which defines it." The second step is "to give fans a message that spreads [...] you have to be a story, as an artist or a label, be remarkable and be worth mentioning." Then, "when this story starts spreading, that's when you start building your ecosystem." The fourth and final step is to use this ecosystem: "once the ecosystem is in place, one should start listening very closely to [...] see what it wants. This is a paradigm-shift in marketing communications, because it has traditionally been about finding a consumer for your product, but this is about finding a product (business opportunity) for your consumers."

Everything he writes makes sense, of course. It may be initially jarring to read about "consumers", "products", and "business opportunities" in the context of music (especially because music, as Grasmayer points out elsewhere, is always also *more* than just a product[5]). But it's true: fans are consumers, an album is a product of sorts, and if it's profit (or even just self-sufficiency) they're after, bands need to look for business opportunities. And, as Grasmayer writes, "the power of an ecosystem in a digital world" is potentially liberating:

> With a strong ecosystem, one also doesn't need to worry about gatekeepers that one traditionally would need, such as the people who decide what to play on MTV... the ecosystem should be like

the cool party happening down the street. ... Soon enough, the party will be attracting people from all over the area ... the fun of the party depends on its own existence and therefore the party protects its continued existence. Now imagine that party without geographical limitations.

Grasmayer's thesis highlights a tension between the democracy and autocracy of music – put another way, the tension between the artist's voice and the commercial impulse. Such a tension isn't universal, but it's always a possibility. For instance: if "finding a product for your consumers" involves changing what you do and the way you do it until you find a way of being that appeals to a large enough group of buyers, isn't it just a variation on the old theme of "selling out", which involves changing your way of being to appease gatekeepers and industry bigwigs? As an artist, how can you reconcile the genuine desire to connect with listeners as people with the need to connect with listeners as customers? How can you reconcile your sense of self with what you know your fans want if or when there seems to be a discrepancy?

I'm reminded of something I read as an undergraduate, studying American politics. In a book called Thinking Points, the linguist George Lakoff uses President Ronald Reagan as a case study for political success of a certain ilk. "Reagan connected with people," Lakoff writes, "he [...] appeared authentic – he seemed to believe what he said." As a consequence: "voters identified with Reagan; they felt he was one of them ... because they believed in the integrity of his connection with them as well as the connection between his worldview and his actions."

I remember thinking, and still think, that there's something funny about the phrase "appeared authentic". Voters trusted Reagan as a leader not necessarily because his beliefs and background matched theirs but because he gave the impression of honesty; he seemed to embody his own values. But appearing to be a certain way does not necessarily mean you are that way; so to appear authentic is by no means to actually be authentic. And it strikes me that if a musician is a businessman, he is also a politician, campaigning for the support of whoever will listen. The relationship between a musician and his fans can quickly become unbalanced; the trick, I suppose, is to find a core group of people with whom your values (musically speaking, in this case) really are aligned, where there's no need to feign or deceive. When I speak to the Squids the thing I feel is that Little Fish have a community that transcends their music. The Squids are rooting for Little Fish, and not just on the off chance that the band becomes famous. They're rooting for all of Little Fish, whatever that turns out to be.

Perhaps the most difficult relationship, though, the trickiest and most volatile, is the one that musicians have with the world. It's the world that makes (or breaks) them, just as they make (or destroy and rebuild, again and again, until something sticks or something dies) their own world. It's the world, usually, that decides the value of things, and it's often the world that inspired the rebellion or instilled the ambition of an artist in the first place. It's the world that the artist must reject, or find a way to win over, find a way to operate within.

In the preface to his book Listen to This, Alex Ross writes of his quest to find out "how a powerful personality can imprint itself on an inherently abstract medium – how a brief sequence of notes or chords can take on the recognizable quirks of a person close at hand." He concludes that, "Maybe the only trait these musically possessed men and women have in common is that they are unlike one another or anyone else. Many are exiles, wanderers, restless searchers. ... One way or another, they unsettle whatever genre they inhabit, making the familiar strange."

Exiles, wanderers, restless searchers. People for whom success, in a broad, conventional sense, is irrelevant, or inevitable, or both. People cast out, or opting out. People on the outside, looking in. I'm reminded of a conversation I had with Spring Offensive guitarist Theo Whitworth. We were winding up after an interview, and we chatted casually for a few minutes about Oxford, our common ground. We talked about a mutual desire to remain, in some senses, outsiders here, even though it's our home, even though we belong: it's a desire to stay just enough on the fringes that it's still possible to have perspective, a vantage point. At the time it seemed like a side note, an incidental exchange, but now I wonder if it was more important than I gave it credit for. It's a romantic way of looking at the creator, and it does nothing to subvert the melodramatic myth of the starving unhappy artist in his ramshackle room, alone but for the urge to make, but there's a sense in which this kind of uneasy relationship to the world is actually beneficial for a person who hopes to build a life out of making things that don't have an easily identifiable, or even a consistent, value.

In the end, though, it's as Throwing Muses frontwoman and singer-songwriter Kristen Hersh writes: "I don't care who you are, the World is not your world. Movie stars imitate you, not the other way around. Movies and books and songs are about small worlds because that's where real life happens. You have passions, your loved ones are your stars, your stories are true, your opinions are valid, you are the only expert when it comes to what you love."[6]

IV. Value

Well, you know, we're talking in a world where guys go down into the mines, chewing coca and spending all day in backbreaking labour. We're in a world where there's famine and hunger and people are dodging bullets and having their nails pulled out in dungeons so it's very hard for me to place any high value on the work that I do to write a song. Yeah, I work hard but compared to what?

— Leonard Cohen

Nature does not give us our livelihood gratis; we must win it by toil of some sort or degree.

— William Morris

The day job. Don't give up your day job, people say, when you tell them, for instance, you're thinking of giving up what looks like a perfectly nice office gig in order to become a full-time writer. The advice is accompanied by a knowing smile. You know what the knowing smile means, because you know all of the ways in which giving up your day job is a bad idea, and you know about all of the people who have failed before you, and about all of the ways in which you, too, will probably fail. But the nature of work itself seems cheapened or changed by the idea of the day job, which is mostly a misnomer anyway – how many nights, too, and weekends, spent crafting emails, fighting fires, worrying about things of very little consequence? Simply in terms of energy, it's a loss: much more goes in than comes out, and what comes out is just a humble paycheque. You trade time; nothing tangible is built or bought.

A common impulse of the musicians I've spoken to in the last year has been to *make*, though the motivation for this desire varies widely (asking people why they make music is a bit like asking why you wake up in the morning, or why you love your family: it isn't an unanswerable question, exactly, but people respond using different, often disparate, vocabularies). It sounds obvious: you wouldn't pluck the strings of a guitar unless you wanted to make a sound. But to reconcile that internal driving force with the harshness of the external world – a world that demands payment, whether in time, sweat, or cash – is a complicated business.

In the world that demands payment, it isn't easy to make for the sake of making. I think of Paul Auster, in *Hand to Mouth*: "Most writers lead double lives. They earn good money at legitimate professions and carve out time for their writing as best they can: early in the morning, late at night, weekends, vacations." ("My problem," Auster adds, "was that I had no interest in leading a double life. It's not that I wasn't willing to work, but the idea of punching a clock at some nine-to-five job left me cold, utterly devoid of enthusiasm.") I think of the five young members of Spring Offensive, all employed full-time in variously humdrum but equally energy-consuming ways; I think of myself as a young post-graduate student, telling people I met at parties that I made photocopies for a living, writing after hours or when everyone in the office had gone to lunch. I think of Leonard Cohen, aged 37, telling an interviewer, "success is survival". It isn't that a double life is necessary for the artist to become whole, like a rite of passage – I think that's bullshit, the sort of thing we like to tell ourselves retrospectively, as comfort or as a warn-ing for would-be-fools-like-us. *Don't quit your day job.* I'm guilty of it, too: I know how to wear the knowing smile. No, the double life is not the only way of life. But it's true: sometimes the day job is necessary for survival.

It's clear that people in pursuit of a career in music will have different goals and different means of achieving them. It's clear, in fact, that people have very different ideas of what "a career in music" means. It may mean, for instance, that you actually derive no income whatsoever from the music you write and perform, but instead from activities around the music: you give guitar lessons, you're a session musician, you play covers at weddings, you build websites for bands, direct music videos, whatever works. In fact the goal may simply be to create a situation in which one is able to prioritize or accommodate comfortably the urge to write or play music, whether or not that music "sells". So perhaps I should speak of "a life in music" rather than "a career in music", and the powerful constructive impulse that seems common amongst people who want a life in music is elastic. It accommodates a variety of beliefs and ambitions, because the ultimate ambition is simply satisfaction in one's work, whether that work is hand-printing a few hundred cards or playing to a stadium of 6,000 people.

In a lecture on "Useful Work versus Useless Toil", delivered in 1884 to the Hampstead Liberal Club, William Morris spoke of "two kinds of work – one good, the other bad".

"[W]orthy work," he suggests, "carries with it the hope of pleasure in rest, the hope of the pleasure in our using what it makes, and the hope of pleasure in our daily creative skill. All other work but this is worthless; it is slaves' work – mere toiling to live, that we may live to toil."

Morris's criteria is still relevant. Despite the advice offered to me by those older and wiser, I did quit my day job, in the end. It was bad work, by Morris's standards. I wasn't making the world a better place, which is something that my ten-year-old self probably thought I might be doing by the time I was old enough to have a career. But worse, an insult on an even baser level: I wasn't making *anything*, except, at times, myself crazy. There was no creative skill required, particularly, although you could well argue that office politics, placating clients, learning the corporate lingo, are skills that require creativity on a major level.

It did have one thing going for it, though, that job: a regular salary. Can you imagine? When I had one, all I could think was how little I needed it: I didn't have any time to spend shopping or eating out, or any energy to go on holiday (and I couldn't bring myself to leave my emails unchecked for a week anyhow). Far better to have my freedom than a positive bank balance. Now that I don't have a salary in the same way (the same amount, deposited into my account on the same day of every month), of course, all I can think is how desperately I would like that boring, comfortable security; I have plenty of time to go shopping and eat out, but no money with which to do either. A holiday is absolutely out of the question, even though it's the one thing I really want, the thing I really think would help. And there you have it: the classic catch-22 of a creative life. Toil to live so that you may live to toil; or else go hungry. Couched in those terms, it sounds melodramatic, and it's true that I'm not hungry. But it's also true that sacrifices have been made.

❧

There is, it should be said, a particular preoccupation with money amongst so-called "creatives". In *Out of Sheer Rage*, Geoff Dyer writes about D. H. Lawrence's "tendency towards niggardliness". Many of Lawrence's letters, Dyer points out, "are long, itemized whinges about how much things are costing, how he is being overcharged, how the exchange rate is working to his disadvantage (especially in Italy), how he had to pay duty on books sent through the post [...] He found it hard work, too, to keep in temper with the various publishers and agents he felt were not treating him honestly." This concern, it turns out, is not a unique quirk of Lawrence's:

> Perhaps we should not make too much of Lawrence and money. He was, after all, a genuinely freelance writer in that he lived entirely by his pen (and the odd loan) and freelance writers are notoriously obsessed with money. I am, at any rate. When Flaubert – who, unlike Lawrence (and me), had a modest private income to live off – declared "everybody is hard up, starting with me!" he was not only lamenting his lot, he was also striking the authentic note of literary single-mindedness. Read most writers' letters and book-writing appears to take a subordinate place to book-keeping.[7]

This last postulation is illustrated by the letters of P. G. Wodehouse, a writer who surely didn't struggle to earn a penny ("spend money like water, because we are simply rolling in it" he writes cheerfully to his wife in 1965; some 30 years earlier he'd written to a friend, "we always did have too much money, and a nest egg of about fifty thousand quid in gilt edged securities is as much as anybody could want"[8]). Wodehouse's letters (and he was a prolific letter-writer) are peppered with references to what he's earned and what he's owed.

I can understand this as a preoccupation, although I'm hardly scrupulous enough to attract the favour of shopkeepers wishing to extend credit, a trait Dyer alleges he shares with Lawrence, and hardly industrious enough to have amassed Wodehouse's "nest egg of about fifty thousand quid". The things most necessary to survival – food, drink, clothing, shelter – cost money, no matter how you go about it. And when you're trading something like words in a book or notes in a song for that money, the transaction, which once, in the warm glow of a contract and a salary, seemed pretty dull, starts to take on the kind of sickening thrill of a roller-coaster ride. As Juju puts it, "I've got nothing against being famous and nothing against making money. You have to make money to pay your rent, to live."

Maybe my own obsession with money is just displaced anxiety – now free, more or less, to structure my time as I wish, which was pretty much the only thing I wanted when I couldn't, I pluck at random from the infinite pool of potential worries a new fixation: my finances. "Dipping into my overdraft" – once a vague, distant possibility, a comfort on a cold night – has become a thing I do more regularly than I pay my rent; it's not so much dipping as drenching myself in the despair of potential insolvency. There are times, when things are going particularly badly or particularly well, for instance, when it seems like all I can talk about is despicable money – and I don't even have Lawrence's or Wodehouse's right to indignation; no one has promised me anything, no one has failed to deliver, no one owes me a penny. It's just a constant background noise, a companion of sorts for long nights and lonely days.

Some evidence of this can be seen in the revelation that, over the course of writing this book, almost every conversation I had with Ben and Juju about being musicians turned, at some point, to money. I blame myself entirely for this, but I also know that it's as substantial a concern for them – and for so many bands and songwriters – as it has been for me. Even from the dubious vantage point of our relative privilege (I lament my sorry state by writing about it on a shiny MacBook Pro, after all) the question of money, of value, sometimes seems to be bigger than all the others, even when it shouldn't be. By talking to Ben and Juju, I am able to ascertain that things get easier with time, but they never really get *easy*, not necessarily. Little Fish have been playing gigs and making noise for years, and as Juju points out, they have made some money, largely through licensing songs to be used in popular video games like *Rock Band* and *Tony Hawk's Pro Skater*. But there's no certainty and no real security, no sense of how things will work out long-term, and one particular question comes up, again and again: *but how are we supposed to make a living?*

The answer to this question is nothing but another question: *what is a living?* It all depends on what you consider a living to be. Obviously what I consider a living to be may be different to what other people consider a living to be. I consider a functioning laptop to be essential to the quality of life I require – while I know that it's hardly necessary for survival in the strict sense of the word. On the other hand, I can't imagine anything I'd like less than to spend hard-earned money on than an expensive car. In a sense, Ben and Juju and I and others like us trade in the currency of freedom: we meet at odd times, in the early afternoon on a Tuesday, when the rest of the city is hard at work, sweating in cubicles or conference rooms. We drink our coffee knowing that, paradoxically, we have time on our sides: although it can sometimes be difficult to understand where the next penny will come from, we have the time to find out. If only you could live on time; if only you could buy pints with time.

In this climate, the idea of sustainability starts to seem increasingly alluring. It certainly sounds like a worthy goal. Why write a book, record an album? Not to become stars, slaves to a system built on doubt and desire, but simply to exist, to keep existing, to stay still. Stagnancy is an ugly word, implying a kind of failure to kick-start or manage one's own life – but so too is *progress*, as in, the myth of progress, the pursuit of a goal that is always just out of reach, no matter where you are, how far you've come. Sustainability seems to allow for the possibility of a life spent creating, not wishing.

For a while, sustainable creativity was my answer to everything. In many ways, it still is. But I also think it's harder than it sounds, and has a broader definition than I first gave it credit for. In 2009, I went to New York with Ben (in his pre-Little Fish days) and my boyfriend, then a freelance web developer/researcher/bartender. We were on a very particular mission: to reduce as far as possible and then recoup the cost of our trip by doing the things we enjoyed (playing music, writing stories, connecting with people who could offer us lodging and a sense, even if for a week, of community). It was not in itself a particularly groundbreaking idea, but we were eager to explore the idea of sustainable creativity – of finding a way, in short, to make for the sake of making. Shortly before we left, I wrote an overview of what we were hoping to achieve:

> We're playing with this idea of "sustainable creativity". It's about using communities and ideas to sustain yourself, so that you're able to do what you love doing. It's simple, on paper: if you're a writer, you find a way to write. If you're a musician, you find the support you need to play gigs and write songs. If you're someone without a clearly defined path, someone who just likes to play with ideas – it means finding a way to do that.
>
> It sounds easy, but it isn't. Creative output takes a lot of time, energy, love, and support, not only from the creator, but also from his or her community. The problem is that many of us are saddled with a lot of extra baggage. We have bills to pay and debts to pay off. We have social and professional obligations that rigidly divide our days. Very likely we're burdened with a "real job" – which we may find intellectually dull and emotionally empty, but necessary

nonetheless (I mostly babysit photocopiers and answer telephones, for instance).

And in an era where time is money, how do you justify spending a few hours every day on your craft? How do you find a few hours every day? It's impossible to underestimate the negative power of financial constraints. If you constantly spend your time thinking, *I should be making money, not fucking around*, you quickly become creatively impotent.

So suppose we make things easier for ourselves. Suppose, to start, we surround ourselves with other, similarly minded, creatively charged people, and become a kind of micro-community based on the idea of mutual inspiration. This removes a number of barriers, and in their places, provides us with a number of opportunities. It gives us an automatic audience, a built-in sounding-board, a kind of creativity support group. It allows for collaborative effort and means that even an ordinary trip to the pub can result in a great idea. In a way, it combines the social aspect of our lives with the creative aspect, thus gaining us time as well as emotional backing.

Well, that's good. That's a source of motivation and stimulation. But we're still stuck with that bland job, those pesky bills, all the worries that get us down. Even if we have a micro-community of like-minded creatives, we're still not going anywhere. Not yet.

The next thing to do, then, is to give up the rock star dream. Forget, for a moment, that you want to be the next superstar of the music, or literary, or art, or whatever world. And remember why you started singing, or writing, or drawing, or playing with ideas, in the first place. Innovative solo bass player Steve Lawson writes prolifically, and very well, about this: "I no longer need to pretend to be a rockstar. The mythology of rock'n'roll is nowhere near as interesting as the reality of creativity." And, Steve adds, "The 80s dream of everyone becoming Stadium rock stars has faded, and more and more musicians are looking at fun ways to get to play music in a financially sustainable way."[9] And what we're trying to say is: not just musicians. Anyone who wants to make anything should be listening to Steve on this point.

It sounds cheesy, but this is an idea about survival and satisfaction, not about making a profit, not about constantly striving, clawing your way up the celebrity hierarchy. This is an idea about how you can do what you love doing – what you would be doing anyway – and earn enough from it to justify doing it as something more than a hobby. To earn enough from it to recoup your costs, eat a meal or two. Eventually, to earn enough from it to pay all those bills, to live comfortably, to buy a new pair of boots when you need to. But to start, it's only about getting by.

Luckily, that built-in creative community – even if it's just a group of two or three people – is the key. Gone are the days when any artist can continue to cling to the alcoholic outcast myth and hope that her lonely genius will be discovered. There's just too much stuff out there for that to be a viable tactic. There are literally thousands of other musicians writing songs and putting them up on the Internet. Thousands of other film-makers uploading clips to YouTube. Thousands of other writers with blogs. Thousands of other painters with thousands of canvases stacked up in their basement. And every single one of them can publicize themselves, advertise themselves, with the click of a button. Passivity and sheer luck may work for some; but the only way to guarantee a sustainable, creative life is to actively seek one out.

So you start with a tiny community. A few friends. Maybe you start at the pub, where ideas can flow unchecked by the ordinariness of daily life. And you realize that actually, there's a lot of overlooked potential in the world. You buy some tickets to New York. You decide that you're going to prove this theory by living it.

So we are three people, with different skills and ambitions but a common goal of creating things and doing cool stuff, taking a week off work. We're going to pack up our guitars, our laptops, our brains, and head across the Atlantic, where we're going to do what we love, and what we're good at, and find a way to survive. We're going to stay cheaply (with friends, on couches). We're going to earn just enough to recoup our travel expenses, and hopefully have enough left over for a few beers at the end of the day.

There are, of course, one or two things that anybody sensible might want to ask — at least, there are some things I had to ask *myself* as I wrote this all down:

But isn't hunger / poverty / whatever a good creative motivator?
Maybe it is, maybe it isn't. But this isn't about "making it" as an artist, necessarily (though it certainly could be); it's about literally surviving off your own work. It's not about becoming great whilst (or even as a result of) stealing bread and sleeping on the street, but about using whatever greatness you already possess to buy bread, pay your rent, and get by. It's simply meant to be proof that you can, if that's what you want to do.

Okay. But by making it as much about money as the creative output itself, aren't you somehow tainting your work? Aren't you basically selling out, on a minute scale?
This is really where the word "sustainability" comes in. This whole idea is fundamentally about sustaining yourself, as a creative-type, so that you can create more. Ultimately it's always about the creative output, and the act of creating, not about the money; the money is simply what allows that process of creation to occur unfettered.

I don't find myself opposed to any of what I wrote in 2009; these are the same issues that Ben and Juju and I continue to discuss, the same fundamental questions about how to build the life you want. It remains a point of pride that we did, in fact, cover the cost of that trip (just — and only because we volunteered to be bumped from our return flight in exchange for £300 vouchers from the airline). But there was something I didn't directly address then, something that doesn't change things, but certainly complicates them: ambition is not always as evil as it seems like it should be, and the desire to be great is sometimes hard to suppress.

In March of 2012, Ben and Juju travelled to Istanbul for a long weekend, to play a few gigs. On their return, Ben wrote the following essay, which he published on his blog:

Lifestyle band

Juju was asked to do a DJ set after the Little Fish gig in
Istanbul. It was her first, and she rocked it. It was the first
time I'd stayed around for a whole DJ set in years. And for
the first time in ages I heard the difference in dynamics,
volume and mastering style between records over a loud
PA.

People have been talking about the Loudness Wars for
years now, and the unfortunate trend of mastering everything painfully loud has mostly passed. We've intentionally made the new Little Fish garage recordings quite sparse
and dynamic rather than loud and punchy. But when we
put one on at the end of the night after everyone had gone
home it didn't sound quite as impressive as a lot of the
other tunes.

This prompted a conversation about whether you should
master stuff loud just so it stands up next to the other songs
on the radio, or in the DJ set. The obvious answer is no,
because you don't want to make recordings that you don't
like. But are you putting yourself at a disadvantage?

As ever, the answer seems to lie in the awkward balance
between DIY and "DIY".The pure DIYer says you shouldn't
even think about it because radio and DJ sets are the tools
of the evil machine and if people discover and love your
music for what it is they won't care. The band who wants
to be DIY but also famous says your track needs to compete
with major label commercial releases.

And this is the problem we face at every turn. If you're a
jazzer or a folkster or a solo bass player I imagine it's quite
easy to make decisions without worrying about whether
your record will sound amazing on Radio 1's Friday night
playlist or in the middle of a DJ set in a rock club in
Istanbul. But as a band on the vaguely mainstream indie-
rock spectrum there's a fame-based outlook baked in to
your world, whether you like it or not. Fans mostly equate

fame with success. Managers always equate fame with success. Rock clubs market their gigs with fame.

If you were a music fan living in Istanbul and didn't know Little Fish, you would have seen our name and photo on posters all around the cool part of town, heard our name and song on the radio (along with our "fame cred" – the list of famous bands we've supported), seen the digital poster and the YouTube "video poster" on Facebook pages and venue websites. All of these things would subtly conspire to make you buy a ticket for the gig and be excited to see this band from the UK.

That's all just good marketing for a well-promoted gig. But marketing and fame are linked, and so if you want to play at the Babylon club you need to engage with the fame game. You need to provide fame-ish photos and music that sounds sufficiently close to famous music that it won't freak people out.

The pure DIYer would suggest that playing rock clubs is just buying into the dying model of an unsustainable industry, and that you'd be better to get out while you can and start promoting your own gigs, preferably in an ironic non-venue with lampshades dotted around the stage.

But how then do you get to travel to Istanbul and play a sold-out gig in the nation's favourite rock club? To spend a day exploring a new city, learning and mispronouncing Turkish words, recording acoustic sessions in hotel bars, meeting interesting people and learning, learning, learning? Because surely that's the whole point? At least it is for us. We make music partly because it's fun and rewarding in itself, but also so we can travel and meet people and have great adventures.

In the tech industry they have a phrase, "lifestyle company", which refers to a small company that covers its costs and allows the owner to live a certain lifestyle. They are generally looked down upon by the swankier start-ups and funding people because they don't aspire to make zillions or be famous. The owners of these companies sustain their lifestyle by making difficult decisions that promote the long-term viability of their company over the short-term gains that massive funding might offer.

We face the same sort of decisions all the time. A radio hit, a random chunk of fame or a pile of money would give us short-term gains. We could reach more people, or afford to spend more time making records. It's what every band used to dream of, and it still sounds amazing. The call of fame is very alluring, even though logically we know it makes no sense. Whenever we talk about how we're so glad to be independent, in control, making the music we want to make, we add "of course, we wouldn't mind a massive hit".

But if the lifestyle companies, the jazzers, the folksters and the solo bass players are anything to go by, the only way to sustain a DIY band long-term is to actively refuse the hits, the fame and the investors. Because as soon as you have those, you have a responsibility to someone other than yourself to make music that is successful on their terms. And that undermines all the reasons why you're doing it in the first place: you're not making the music you want any more, you suddenly have to work with someone else's expectations and the lifestyle you've created disappears.

So I suppose what we're doing is trying to find a compromise, to engage with the machine just enough to achieve our goals of travel and adventure and musical expression but to do it on our own terms, without compromising the things we care about. It's not easy, and the perfect balance is different for everyone (and changes over time), but talking about it openly makes the decisions easier to understand.

That caveat – "we wouldn't mind a massive hit" – grates on me and comforts me in equal measure. I remember the epiphany I had one November, the thing that struck me as being so profoundly true: that I didn't want my own, writerly equivalent of a massive hit for the *sake* of having a massive hit, just so that I could continue to do the things I loved doing. Well, I'm not aiming for a Pulitzer, but I wouldn't mind. The thing that grates me about it is what seems, from the surface, to be a lurking hypocrisy – as if it's all well and good to champion sustainability, to declare oneself independent and innocent, but only until or unless an opportunity for greatness, in a grander, more conventional sense, presents itself.

A week or so after Ben wrote this, we spoke about it. We met for a coffee on a miserable afternoon, the rain coming down outside, the temperature disagreeably balmy. He and Juju were making some last-minute preparations for the three-week tour of China they were about to embark on – a tour that would only just break-even, the ultimate example of playing music "to travel and meet people and have great adventures". In conversation, I was alternatively aggressive and empathetic: "So fame is the goal again, then?" I said, as if I had somehow been betrayed. But I knew it was not so simple, and I had not been betrayed – if anything, I had been caught out, taken by surprise by the apparition of an idea I hadn't yet been able to articulate. In my understanding of the idea of sustainable creativity, there had never really been anything to preclude massive mainstream success. You may rationally know that you don't need a hit just to get by, but how do you bleed yourself dry of the ambition to be heard by thousands, maybe millions, of people?

So the question becomes something like: *can we string a tightrope between A Massive Hit and DIY Sustainability and walk it? For how long can we balance before we fall to one side or the other – or is balancing, in itself, a sustainable act?*

When Ben and Juju and I first conceived of this book as an idea, I vaguely envisaged it as a kind of handbook – not exactly a "how-to", but a manifesto, a guide to making music (or anything, really) in such a way that subverted the idea that fame or fortune was the ultimate goal but still allowed you to live off what you loved, not what you got stuck doing when you ran out of steam. I don't believe this is a naïve view; I believe that it's a sensible one, and there are many fine examples of it at work. But there are a million shades of grey, and as Ben says, sometimes the hard part is not to stand aggressively on one side of an invisible line or the other, but to find some overlap, to inhabit the space opened up by compromise. "So fame is the goal again, then?" I ask, and the answer, I guess, is that it never really was the goal, but if it's the by-product of something else, who's going to complain?

One of the things that makes it so particularly difficult to live off music is that it's difficult to determine where, exactly, the value is. When you buy music (in whatever form: MP3, vinyl, gig tickets), what are you actually buying? On one level, you're buying the music itself, the song or set of songs, and all the emotional, spiritual, physical, or intellectual pleasure or stimulation that song or set of songs gives you. You're buying any memories that are or will be associated with the songs. There's also any physical object that contains or connects to the music: liner notes, a plastic CD case, a USB stick, a cartoon. With a gig, there's the spectacle, the experience. And so on.

But all of these things mean ostensibly different things to different people. Some people consider a gig to be worth paying much more for. Others consider it a waste of time and money: with a recording, you can listen as many times as you want, have the band eternally in your ears if you want; the gig is too ephemeral. A download of a track that has no corporeal form is even more nebulous: when you click "purchase", you're essentially buying just the sound itself.

Often, of course, you're not buying anything. You're streaming, borrowing, stealing, even downloading for free on behest of the artist himself. No money changes hands – a contentious fact but not always a bad thing for artists, particularly those who have begun to shift their ideas about what people want to buy from a musician. "Get over the idea that your success is equated with selling the right to listen, or selling control over when people listen," writes Seth Godin. "Relinquish the opportunity to make money by controlling who can listen and when. That's gone. It's over [...] What you can sell, what you better be able to sell, is intimacy. It's interactions in public. Souvenirs. Limited things of value. Experiences. Memories."[10] Or, as Andrew Dubber puts it (in a nod to Christopher Small*), "Music's not a thing we can hold in our hands, or own."[11] It's an activity, requiring human participation and interpretation – "a verb rather than a noun," as Dubber writes in an email to me.

So it's inherently hard to ascribe value to things like music and literature. It may seem that some works of art are unquestionably great, even though you might struggle to affix a monetary value to "great". But

---

* Small wrote that, "Music is not a thing at all but an activity, something that people do. The apparent thing 'music' is a figment, an abstraction of the action, whose reality vanishes as soon as we examine it at all closely." (Small, Christopher. Musicking: The Meanings of Performing and Listening. Wesleyan University Press, 1998, p2).

subjectivity means that even this can be (and probably will be) disputed – there's Evelyn Waugh, for instance, author of one of my favourite novels, writing about Joseph Heller's *Catch-22*, another of my favourites: "It suffers not only from indelicacy but from prolixity [...] You are mistaken in calling it a novel."[12]

But money is, nevertheless, supposedly an indicator of value, to some extent. It's "the World's favorite measuring stick", as Kristen Hersh calls it, writing of the struggle to marry external valuations with personal ones: "My band also carried a very low price tag: the World didn't value our world. Not enough people cared enough about our music to allow us to play it for a living any more. This was confusing, as our band was ubiquitous to us. It was like someone telling you that your left arm wasn't cool enough."[13]

Making something that you find valuable is not the same thing as making something that other people find valuable; and even if other people do find it valuable, that value will not necessarily be translated into dollars and dimes. Money may be the world's favorite measuring stick, but it isn't necessarily the best language for appreciation.

So how do you make a living – or even a bit of money – as a musician? I can tell you how you don't, anyway. In August of 2011, Ben and Juju went to Leicester to play a gig; I was corresponding with Ben via email about the book at the time, and asked him how the gig had gone. I'd seen some mention, online, of a possible mix-up, but it was just a tiny gig in a place I'd never been – I figured I'd get a one-line response. It turned out to be one of the most inadvertently fruitful questions I could have asked:

On Saturday, 27 August, 2011 at 02:05 AM,
Miranda Ward wrote:

Hi –
Good to hear your thoughts on the 'why' of musicmaking.
Sure I'll have a more interesting response when more
awake.

Also interested in this idea of up/down (e.g. 'on the way up') — which is obviously dependent on a shared (cultural) understanding of which way is up and which way is down. But what if we decide that playing music in a garage is up and owning lots of shit is down?

How was the gig tonight? Saw online that the venue had been listed incorrectly? A consequence of too many middle men? Hope it went well anyway — an opportunity to reach a few new fans, perhaps.

M

**On Saturday, August 27, 2011 at 1:28 PM,
Ben Walker wrote:**

So last night's gig was hilariously symptomatic of the awkward industry limbo in which we're suspended. I'll tell you about it, partly because it's interesting to think about and partly because it's just funny. It all started with an email from Jules to our agent:

> **Subject: Leicester Show ??**
>
> *Hi,*
>
> *How are you?*
>
> *This gig just appeared on Songkick: [link]*
>
> *Apparently it's an "Early show 2pm till 5pm".*
>
> *Does anyone know anything about it?*
>
> *I have no idea.*
>
> *Please can we be told about a show before it goes public! This makes it all very confusing. It would*

be great if we could have more communication and work together on things.

Ju X

The agent replied that it had been confirmed as an evening show with our manager a week or so before. He must have forgotten to tell us. A Little Fish gig on Songkick automatically shows up on our site, so I edited the notes to take out the 2pm—5pm nonsense and forgot about it.

Somewhere along the way the promoter switched the venue. The venue name quietly changed in the emails we got from our agent, but because we'd never been to Leicester they meant nothing to us and we didn't notice. So the wrong venue was listed on our site up until about 9pm yesterday, when I noticed on Twitter that @kuangeleven was racing round all the venues in Leicester trying to find out where we were playing.

I'll backtrack a little. We don't know anyone in Leicester and we'd never played there before, so we weren't expecting much of an audience. In the end two people came to see us, and the support band and their girlfriends stayed for our set. We were promised £80 and paid £75, of which £40 went on petrol. That leaves £11.67 each. We were given a "buyout", which means the promoter gives you some cash to buy your own meal instead of feeding you. That was £20 between 4 of us (Nez's wife was there too). The meal cost £40, so we each put in an extra fiver. So Jules, Nez and I came home with £6.67 each. Probably less, because I bought at least two coffees, a coke and a bag of Maltesers. T probably broke even.

Yes, we sold four t-shirts (even the sound man bought one!). Yes, we got half a dozen emails for the list. But when you look at it objectively it's insane. Absolutely insane. Let's step back a little further.

There are a few different reasons to play a gig. You might

want to promote a new release. You might want to make some money. You might just want to get your name out to a new audience. We did none of these last night. The gig was booked, along with a few similar gigs in the last week, to make it seem like our agent does something. Given that she only makes 10% of our fee, I can't imagine getting £7.50 for organising a gig is her prime motivation. Last night's gig was an exercise in bureaucratic futility.

We did four gigs on this "tour". Two of the gigs were organised by Little Fish fans, one in Reading and one in Cheltenham. They got in touch with our agent, who in both cases failed to respond. So they emailed us directly, we agreed to do the shows and told our agent to sort it out. The other two gigs were organised by our agent (Cardiff and Leicester).

Cheltenham was organised by Olly, who runs his dad's shoe shop and plays guitar. He put on the gig without making any money. His band played the first support slot. His girlfriend ran the door. He got it listed and mentioned in the local papers, two local radio stations, posters all over town and flyers in the music shops. He organised an acoustic gig for us in the local independent record store in the afternoon and hung out with us until the evening. There were about 40 people at the gig. He gave us the entire takings from the door, which was £180. We sold about £60 of merch.

Reading was organised by Emily, who is fifteen. FIFTEEN! It was an all-day festival in a grungey rehearsal studio on an industrial estate not far from the Reading Festival site, with a dozen local bands playing and Little Fish headlining. Emily is a singer/songwriter and played an early afternoon slot. There were about 50 people at the gig, and we got a fixed fee of £200. We sold about £60 of merch and signed up about 20 people to our mailing list.

Cardiff was organised by our agent. We supported a Brooklyn band called She Keeps Bees. They were awesome,

and we bought their vinyl album for £15. It was a 2.5 hour
drive and we were paid £50 between 4 (Ned played bass),
which didn't quite cover the travel costs (it's £11.50 to
get over the Severn Bridge in a small van). We sold no
merch and signed nobody up to our mailing list.

Leicester was organised by our agent. We played to an
empty room, and even our Leicester fan couldn't get his
friends to come because he didn't know where we were
playing. We stayed and chatted to our two fans and the
sound guy for an hour and miraculously sold £40 of merch.
We signed up the support band to our mailing list. We were
paid £75 and came home with nothing.

Maybe I'm being cynical, but it seems like there might be
a pattern there. When people care, the gig is good. When
they don't, it's not.

Needless to say, we're on a mission to sack our agent now.
Again. And once we've done that we'll move on to the press
people, who we're paying A THOUSAND POUNDS A MONTH for no
reason whatsoever.

In other, more positive news, we're really excited about
starting something new, and Jules is getting into the idea
of creating a manifesto for the new Little Fish. Watch
this space...

Ben

I'd been speaking to Ben and Juju for months about the logistics of being
in a band, but even so, Ben's email was a bit of a revelation for me.
There's no reason it should have been – I was three months into my own
freelance career at that point, and knew damn well that what you think
is going to make you money is not, in fact, what's going to make you
money. But it was a revelation nonetheless, or at least a very stark example of the hurdles a band regularly faces, a strong illustration of precisely
why it's so often so hard to marry needs and desires.

The truth is, I don't have an easy answer to the question of how any of us is going to make a living. I don't have an answer, either, to the question of how you can monetize music in a way that doesn't compromise whatever values you're unwilling to compromise, mainly because the idea of "monetizing" anything sounds so awkwardly corporate that I can't imagine how it applies to the world I want to inhabit.

There are plenty of possible answers, of course. There are plenty of things that have worked and plenty of things that might work. That's what makes "this" – whether you mean this week, this year, this decade, this ambiguous era – such an exciting time for music. There's Amanda Palmer, for instance, proclaiming crowdfunding website Kickstarter "the future of music".[14] She raised over a million dollars – nearly ten times more than her already substantial $100,000 target – for a record, art book, and tour. On the subject of crowdfunding, the bassist Steve Lawson, an independent musician who's managed quite admirably to cobble together a living for himself, writes:

> Part of Kickstarter (and Pledge Music)'s success comes from the permission it gives people to get excited about The Big Project, rather than being stuck with the old model that paying for music is about getting a product and the stories around music are the stuff that goes in magazines so that we know when the product will be available. Now, we can see the recordings as a document of music-making, as something to enjoy, to soundtrack our lives with, to tell stories with and be told stories by. And we can be part of any number of those stories.[15]

So, for some, there's hope that a solution is upon us. It might just work: to wrest control away from the world, to challenge the idea that you must pay for something only after it's been created. I like the idea that part of the appeal of something like crowdfunding is to pay not just for product but for process; to give the punter some role to play in the production of an album (or indeed a book). I like the fluidity of the model that Lawson describes, where a recording can be seen as simultaneously a story in itself and a part of some larger story – where it functions both as process *and* product, in a sense.

But, as Ian Bogost asks in an article for *Fast Company*, "what if Kickstarter is more about the experience of kickstarting than it is about the finished products?"[16] That's often at least partly what Kickstarter and platforms like it are about, and it's not a bad thing on its own, at least not necessarily. But I wonder if the strength of an object's story is diminished if more emphasis is placed on one aspect of that story than another – if, for instance, we are more excited about the act of participating in an album's creation than we are about the album itself. This kind of unbalanced valuation is, after all, hardly more than a reversal of the traditional model, in which story and depth are important only insofar as they can help sell more albums.

To emphasise his point, Bogost describes his relationship to a pen he pre-ordered from Kickstarter. "It's nice, I guess," he writes, "but I'm still using a $2 roller-ball to sketch notes in my Moleskine. Yet the Pen Type-A is more than a $100 metal pen that never gets used, it's a memento of the excitement I felt after first seeing the product." His conclusion is that "we don't really want the stuff. We're paying for the sensation of a hypothetical idea, not the experience of a realized product. For the pleasure of desiring it." I don't disagree – the pleasure of desiring something is sometimes pleasure enough – but I also don't see why one can't pay for "the sensation of a hypothetical idea" and "a realized product".

What I do see is that crowdfunding, "pay what you think it's worth", and other similarly innovative structures for supporting artists are not the solution, though they may well be a solution for some people. Because if it's difficult to determine what exactly people are buying when they buy music – sound, memory, a USB stick? – it's even more difficult to determine what people are making when they make music. There's the musician as creator, the musician as performer, the musician as businessperson, the musician as politician – and now, too, the musician as purveyor-of-desire. And to place a specific value on any one aspect of a musician's output (the narrative, the relationship, the live performance, the album, the single song that sends a chill down your spine) – let alone on the Thing As A Whole, whatever that might be – is almost impossible.

Answers and questions, then, are perhaps the wrong way of looking at the issue of what a living is and how to make it. We can only know this: no matter what, no matter how forward-thinking you are, or how well-loved, or how tenacious, there's always the ominous pressure of daily life, and the possibility that the weight will eventually be too great. "When people care, the gig is good. When they don't, it's not," Ben writes, and I think in the end this is the key, the most important thing: if the musician cares, if the listener cares, then it's going to be okay, though no one can say exactly what "okay" means in every case. The likelihood that the weight will eventually become unbearable is equalled by the likelihood that it will lift. And meanwhile the sun comes up, the rain comes down, the post arrives, the bills drop like stones through the letterbox, and the world keeps spinning.

v. Doing It Yourself

The man who works recognizes his own product in the World that has actually been transformed by his work; he recognizes himself in it, he sees in it his own human reality, in it he discovers and reveals to others the objective reality of his humanity, of the originally abstract and purely subjective idea he has of himself.

– Alexandre Kojéve

October. Ben and Juju have just finished playing a short set in an independent record shop on Oxford's Cowley Road. They've recently released their single *Wonderful*, produced by Gaz Coombes. And they're at that point in a performance where the band become salesmen, peddling wares. They mention the single – rows of the vinyl version are on display in the shop, and it's available for download online.

"Oh, and we made our own apple juice," Juju says, holding up a green glass bottle emblazoned with the band's logo. "It's £4, if you want to buy some."

A ripple of delighted laughter spreads through the crowd. I can confidently say that this is the first time I've seen a band tout home-made apple juice, though I'm not naïve enough to believe that there isn't a precedent. There's always a precedent, and anyway, bands are plugging t-shirts and CDs and gigs all the time. Why not apple juice?

"Yeah," she says, as if warming to the crowd's own warmth. "We can't get the radio to play our songs, you know. But fuck the radio. We've got apple juice!"

❧

**On Tuesday, August 23, 2011 at 8:31 PM,
Ben Walker wrote:**

Miranda,

I was listening to Jonathan Coulton and Merlin Mann
chatting on a podcast earlier and JoCo was talking about
how he started by doing everything himself, and gradually
involved other people (an assistant, and eventually a
manager, booking agent, producer and band). In the beginning he communicated directly with his audience and only
introduced extra layers to the process when it was practically necessary, financially viable and when he had found
people he could trust.

It's almost the opposite trajectory to Little Fish's
current journey from Custard to DIY. The extra layers were
never necessary (but never questioned), never financially
viable and not built on trust. And now we're shedding them
one by one, heading towards a situation where we record
and produce everything ourselves and communicate directly
with our audience.

Food for thought, eh?

Ben

**On Wednesday, August 24, 2011 at 20:21 PM
Miranda Ward wrote:**

Ben,

Interesting — it's similar to the idea we've discussed
previously, that Little Fish is moving in a direction that
the undiscerning observer might describe as "backwards"
— that is to say, in the rock'n'roll myth (whatever that
is), a band starts out in a hometown, outgrows the hometown, leaves, grows distant (often both geographically and
emotionally) from the fans, and achieves success, whereas

of course you're coming home, "shedding the extra layers", making it about the music again. So in a lot of ways what Little Fish is doing is counterintuitive. In other ways maybe it's the only logical thing a band can do, if "band" means "group of people that write/play music for an audience (even if that audience is only each other)".

[...]

Also — since I seem to be preoccupied by the idea of "work" lately — I think there's something interesting about the idea of DIY — about the compulsion to do some-thing constructive with your hands (literally — playing music, but also figuratively — constructing a fan base, being involved in the production of a t-shirt or a tea towel). Isn't it so easy to feel separate from things nowadays? Yesterday evening I took a nap and when I woke up I felt so disconnected from everything that I had a panic attack on my way to the pool. There are lots of reasons that I might have been feeling odd, but it did at one point occur to me to wonder if I would feel differ-ently if, say, I felt more connected to the things I wrote — what if I wrote with a pen and paper? What if I had a printout of a manuscript, to mark up and feel the weight of? What if, for that matter, I even had a printer that functioned?

May have lost the plot a little in that last paragraph. Luckily there isn't really a plot!

M

On Friday, August 26, 2011 at 02:34 AM, Ben Walker wrote:

Miranda,

Having spent the entire day FILING, I haven't really had a chance to [...] think much about anything.

But we just played a gig in a rehearsal room on an industrial estate in Reading, and your words about seeming to
move backwards were ringing in my ears ... The whole thing
was a mad rush and we couldn't hear anything on stage, but
of course nobody in the audience knew or cared that this
was a small, crappy gig for us. We talked to a load of
people afterwards, got mailing list addresses, sold
t-shirts and met some great new fans. If we were on the
way up, climbing the ladder towards a dream career of
Ferraris and champagne, it would have been a textbook gig.

On the way home we talked about why we all do music. We're
not sure. I think we each have different reasons, and it
depends whether you're talking about conscious life
decisions or reasons buried in our infant psyche. I think
I just found something I could do that let me impress,
amuse and socialise with people without having to talk to
them. My brother likes to show off, but is also stubborn
enough to be a drummer just to prove a point (he could
have done pretty much anything). Jules reckons she just
wanted to be different.

Your plot wasn't too lost in your last paragraph. I think
the connectedness of playing gigs is very important to us.
When we feel disconnected because we're just emailing and
project managing all day, we get depressed and life seems
awful and we start to resort to buying things to make life
nicer. Then eventually we play a gig and connect with
people and it all makes sense again. You should definitely
read that book about working with your hands. It will tell
you nothing new, but at least you'll stop worrying that
you're missing something. ;)

OK. Post-gig hyperactivity completely gone now. Just
didn't want to miss a day. Good night.

Ben

After I left my job, in 2011, I was adrift for awhile. I had been hoping that the answer to a question I hadn't yet asked would present itself, like a coin on the pavement or a full moon, stark and bright. It was summer, and the evenings were long, which made the days themselves feel long too, like each of the 24 hours had been stretched just a little. I took to swimming, almost every day, almost obsessively. The ritual of leaving the house, walking to the pool, became the focal point of my otherwise aimless days. Partly it was to impose some sense of structure in my life: the pool, after all, had opening hours, and lanes, and rules. But mainly, I think, it was the physicality of it that brought me back day after day: the exertion, the sensation, the discomfort of the cold water erased almost immediately by the pleasure of moving through it.

One day in August I sat at my desk for hours, writing words but getting nowhere. I sent a dozen emails, or a few, at least. I gave things a bit of thought and deleted a number of the words that I'd taken the time to write earlier. I watched the responses to my own emails come in, each one necessitating some action or response. These are all important things to do, in a day, but progress, if it was indeed happening, was not at all palpable; the phrase "one step forward, two steps backward" occurred to me. The light outside was pale and grey. I got up and had a nap: I told myself that this was the only productive thing to do, to escape, to rest, to clear my mind. And after my nap it was time for my swim. So I left the house, taking my usual route. Along the way I began to feel a bit odd, a bit ill. I felt like I was floating, not walking – drifting down busy streets, invisible, uprooted. I experienced the beginnings of what a doctor had once described to me as a panic attack. It was a surprise; I hadn't felt anything like this for a long time, and I'd felt calm earlier – not even frustrated, just resigned. But it shouldn't have been a surprise. All those aimless days had been leading up to this moment, had culminated in the realization that in my obsessive quest to discover how to make a living doing what I loved, I'd neglected to actually make anything at all. My emphasis on the material aspects of a living – the finances, the grim business of paying rent or train fares or my tab at the pub – had led me down a strange road, and now here I was, feeling like I had little understanding of how to make either money or myself happy, let alone both at once.

The next day I wrote an email to Ben, ostensibly about something else – but my sense of unease seeped in, and I couldn't resist asking, as casually as I could manage: *isn't it so easy to feel separate from things nowadays?* I wondered if it was because I had no way to measure my work, no tangible evidence of my mental exertion. The panic attack I had on the way to the pool had been precipitated as much by this as by anything else (worries about money, say, or the hazy future, all the classic culprits). I was spending hours every day and I had nothing to show for it except for text on a screen – text, moreover, that lived in some nebulous place I sometimes saw referred to as The Cloud, a non-place, really, an imaginary world, a thing I couldn't quite wrap my head around. I briefly contemplated regressing and taking up pen and paper. But the problem was not so simple, I knew. The problem was not really even a problem at all. It's not that words on a page, or notes in your ears, aren't enough: it's that if you spend too much time pondering the weight of your creative output, you're liable to descend quickly into the abyss of Self Pity, where everything you do seems meaningless. What's the point of making something unmeasurable? It's a pointless question, but I did sometimes have irrational fantasies about doing something more obviously constructive for a living: learning to garden, to build fences or pour concrete. Sometimes I envied the bin men as I saw them passing down the street, even though I would make a terrible bin man.

❦

I keep reading about the supposed resurgence of vinyl, in articles with headlines like "Digital Music Created the Resurgence in Vinyl" and "Vinyl resurgence giving a new spin to independent record stores". In fact vinyl only accounted for 0.3% of total music sales in 2011 – hardly a staggering number. But sales of vinyl LPs that year rose by 43.7%,[17] which is a much more impressive figure. When Little Fish released their single *Wonderful*, they released only a vinyl and a digital version, as if the novelty and physicality of the former and the convenience of the latter cancelled out the need for the production of a CD. The CD is still technically king – data from 2011 indicates that it's the UK music buyer's preferred format (it accounts for 76.1% of total sales). But there's something compelling about the argument that, as digital album sales increase,[18] so too does our desire for nostalgic objects like vinyl LPs, things that link us to an otherwise elusive past (one internet meme shows a picture of a cassette tape and a pencil: "our children will never know the link between the two," reads the caption).

In what I recently heard referred to as "the post-Myspace age", the distribution of music online is no longer remarkable; we take for granted that whole albums can be obtained or streamed at the click of a button. So we don't *need* a physical vehicle for a song, but that doesn't mean we don't still sometimes want one. I, for one, am grateful to have been able to dispose of my CD collection, including the cracked jewel cases, the ungainly plastic towers. But I acknowledge, too, the possibility that to strip an album of its packaging is to lose something essential, sometimes. I can hardly remember the last time I deliberately listened to an entire album, let alone to the songs in the order in which they were intended to be heard – everything's on shuffle all the time, all mixed up. I don't know how to affix a value to this, and I don't think I'd want to, because it seems a pretty irreversible change. We listen to music differently – not all of us, not all the time, but generally, and inevitably. Is it good? Is it bad? It just is.

Musicians, though, or a certain breed of them, are enterprising creatures. Some of them are producing not just virtual albums that exist piecemeal in a virtual space but actual *stuff*. They're hand-knitting USB covers, hand-stitching canvas bags for CDs – even, in spite of the supposed obsolescence of the cassette, recording EPs over old tapes purchased in bulk from charity shops. And perhaps this playfulness or physicality is indicative of a wish to recapture or even reinvent the story that comes with an album, to make materials – paper, plastic, vinyl, whatever – matter again, to be involved in an active way in the creation of something. As Matthew Crawford writes in *The Case for Working with Your Hands*: "The satisfactions of manifesting oneself concretely in the world through manual competence have been known to make a man quiet and easy."

Quiet and easy are not always the best qualities for a band, of course, and I suspect that there's also a lot of value in the tension between the abstract and the physical aspects of creation. After weeks or months of empty toil, of emailing, filing, counting t-shirts, it's cathartic to engage with receptive human beings; there's the release Ben describes, the moment when "we play a gig and connect with people and it all makes sense again." No amount of stitching, knitting, or letterpress printing can replace those moments, but it can make the periods between them more bearable. In an interview, Juju tells me the hardest part of being a musician is "the waiting": waiting, she says, for other people to do things, to respond to requests or ideas. So the doing is a way of ameliorating the agony of the waiting. Wait long enough and you may well decide to just do it yourself – whatever "it" is.

The idea of DIY, as a sort of abstract concept, has certainly been the subject of many recent conversations and writings about the future of music as a business. At a forum on "DIY Mainstream" (an ambiguous title if ever there was one), Fred Bolza, VP of Marketing Services at Sony Music Entertainment, spoke about the ways in which his label hopes to take inspiration from DIY culture. Labels, he said, need to shift from being record companies to being "services of value" for artists; we need to stop thinking about records as being the product, he proclaimed, and think instead in terms of "units of art". It was a bit too slick – he was a youngish, casually dressed guy, with hipster hair and an almost-sincere smile, apparently trying to appeal to a demographic someone had identified as "inclined towards DIY but impressionable nonetheless" – but it was only after the forum that I began to identify my feelings of doubt. In the moment, watching him gesture, sip his water, speak eloquently enough on what the mainstream moguls have to learn from the DIY pioneers, I was nodding along, thinking, *this makes sense!* and even, *well, good for the record labels, maybe they're really learning something.* I remembered a quote from a *Guardian* article I'd recently read: "That DIY spirit has just become the norm [...] Artists and people in the music game don't have to rely on that old record label infrastructure; people are just coming together, working collaboratively and doing it for themselves." [19]

But an hour later, after brief disheartening conversation with an NME writer (his vocabulary was loaded with words like "stars", "legends", "worship"), I remembered that what "artists and people in the music game" are tangled up in is not just a bulky infrastructure but a dangerous mindset. Icons, epic gigs, the irony and tragedy of fame: it's all still too alluring to ignore. There's still a rigidity to the way we talk about music. People politely enquiring about the subject of my book, for instance, often ask, when I tell them it's ostensibly about a band, whether or not they'll have heard of the band I'm writing about. *Have they made it? Are they famous? Does the mainstream press care about them?* "We are in the last years of a huge empire, one that was beholden to a myth woven around the miracle of amateurs becoming icons," writes the musician Louis Barabbas. [20] I hope he's right, but even if he is, even if the empire really is in its twilight years, there's still a lot of work to be done; there are still a lot of attitudes to shift. When I talk to Juju about the rewards of being a musician, she tells me that one of her favourite parts of the whole process is the moment she finishes writing a song – a transient moment, and a very private one. But, she adds, this isn't the most intuitive – or most popular – answer. "I think some people get really excited by the things that might obviously be the most rewarding things, like touring with Blondie or Courtney Love. But actually that's just stuff you can say so people will take you a bit more seriously – like speaking a language that they understand." And that language is rooted in a mythology that won't go away just because some cool dude from Sony smiles and tells a room full of people that his label thinks those crazy DIY-ers are actually on to something.

For one thing, what we mean when we talk about "DIY", especially in the context of music, is not always easy to generalize – which perhaps explains why diehard independent musicians and representatives from major record labels are equally happy to use the term. There's a distinction to be made, for instance, between things that are scraped together independently out of pure necessity and things that are made to feel as if they embody the DIY spirit but haven't been created wholly in sympathy with it. One approach is not necessarily better than the other, but sometimes DIY is not so much a rebellious spirit as a kind of aesthetic, a subgenre of "inauthentic authenticity"[21] – like the popular smartphone application Instagram, which allows you to manipulate a digital photograph you took five minutes ago and give it the appearance of a 1970s polaroid. Sometimes it's a lifestyle, a deliberate choice, a big fuck you to The Man. Sometimes it's just the only way to get things done: not a political statement but a simple statement of intent.

In any case, the "do" in the phrase "do it yourself" does imply some perceptible action. And whether you're creating a community or a poorly recorded, hand-decorated EP (or both), there's an end product. Stripped of any more political or historical associations, DIY seems to me to be a spirit that opposes the sluggishness of the shiny machine – all the waiting, meeting, waiting, meeting. The lure of DIY, in its simplest form, is immediacy and independence; it simplifies the relationship between creator and listener, brings them closer together. And to me, Little Fish embody that particular aspect of the DIY spirit, despite their dalliance with Custard/Universal and Juju's insistence that, although "the industry [...] tends to exploit those people," "being signed, it does a lot of good".

Above all, it's Juju's desire for action that's always driven the band. In 2010, when they were in negotiations with their label, and nothing much was happening, and they had months to kill, she and Ben decided to send out gifts to their fans. They asked anyone who was interested in receiving what the band ambiguously referred to as "fishy paper squares" to sign up on the Little Fish website and provide a mailing address – and so The Original Little Fish Paper Club was formed.

In May the band posted the first paper squares to fans around the world. The paper square was actually a booklet, bound by red thread. It had been stitched, addressed, and stamped by hand. It contained colour illustrations by a friend of Juju's, along with words by Juju herself, some vague ("sometimes it was the silence that I believed"), others clear enough ("I've just met someone I like. Should I spare us the pain?"), but all open to interpretation, as if each paper square was a private conversation or interaction between band and recipient. It had nothing and everything to do with the music that the band played or didn't play. It was a story – maybe fictional, maybe not – parts of which were impenetrable, other parts of which were weirdly accessible. There was an appealing greyness, an innocence tinged with heavy worldliness that gave you the impression you were being allowed to see something new or rarely revealed, even if you didn't know exactly what it was.

It was a gimmick, in a sense, but a good one: a way of closing a distance, creating a community around some crazy, half-formed idea. It was something to do while the band waited. And it was a way for Juju and Ben to work with other artists and friends to make something more concrete than the music, something that required a bit of menial labour to produce. A physical object: a thing for people to hold, display, discard.

Over the next two years, Little Fish sent out seven more paper squares. It proved a popular idea – after the first two, the band decided to charge a small subscription fee to cover printing and postage costs, which is how they came to form The New Original Little Fish Paper Club. There were booklets, a letterpress printed card with lyrics to the single *Wonderful*, a comic book, a monoprinted illustration of a fox. The mono-print is interesting: it's odd, offbeat, just a fragile piece of paper on which appears the almost childish form of the fox. Monoprinting is so called because the process allows you to make only one original copy of a print at a time, so every member of the Paper Club received a completely unique print. Though they're all of the same essential thing, there are subtle variations in lines and expressions (on mine, the paper appears smudged, and the fox gazes warily but almost sweetly at who-ever gazes back; on another, made just for fun, the fox wears a jaunty hat). Scratched along the side are the words "Reasons to be fearful" –

just a fragment, something that means nothing. On the back Juju has written: "We're given reason to be fearful, up to you to make the most of it" and signed her name, but even this context provides no elucidation, not really. You wouldn't necessarily look twice at the print, except perhaps with mild curiosity, if you didn't know the story, or some of the story. You may not even look twice at it now that you do know the story: the point of the paper club, as I understand it, was never to create something permanent or even lasting. Just to create *something*, or, rather, some *thing*. The music, intangible as it may be (and by music I mean both story and sound), is the lasting thing, if anything is a lasting thing. The fox (is he the thing to fear or a fearful creature just like you or I?) is a fleeting part of it – a manifestation of some abstract impulse or desire, or just a cute little drawing on a slip of paper.

❧

As part of the process of closing the distance between performer and audience, "doing it yourself" also often eliminates or at least weakens the greedy middleman. There's something deeply empowering about the idea that it might no longer be necessary for some complicated configuration of A&R people, press people, pluggers, and producers to manipulate and take ownership of an album before it ever reaches fans. The internet has created an environment in which, via crowdfunding sites like Kickstarter or PledgeMusic or simply on their own steam, any artist has the opportunity to connect directly with potential listeners. What this means is that a band, with no ties to the industry, no external support or other advantages, recording in their basement, can now theoretically harness the power of a community, whether it's one rooted in a specific city or scattered across the globe, communing only online, and build whatever it is they need to build: a fund for recording, an even bigger community, a road out of obscurity. It can work beautifully, as this very book proves: without the backing of nearly 500 friends, Little Fish fans, and supporters, it wouldn't have been made – but thanks to your contributions and faith, here it is, in your hands.

With crowdfunding, the sky is ostensibly the limit; profit actually reaches the artist, instead of being siphoned off. The rock'n'roll myth has been democratized: fame, or at least sustainability, is no longer a possibility just for the lucky few.

"It sells you a dream," Juju tells me, when I ask her about her own experience with the inverted-commas "industry". "It's a good sales pitch. And I believed it. I wholly believed it." But the democratized, DIY world sells you a dream, too, albeit a potentially more humble one, if it's something more humble you're looking for. Maybe it isn't selling you fame — though it obviously is for some (from a *Guardian* article on crowdfunding and music: "Getting her album made thanks to her fans is the first step, Miss Stylie says, on a path to world domination"[22]). Maybe it's just selling you the idea that you can make money — some money, any money, ten pounds, say, or a hundred — from your music. And maybe — probably, if you're any good — you can. The success stories are heartening, anyway. Take "internet rock star" Jonathan Coulton, who's unsigned, unlikely to get much radio play, but who nevertheless made nearly $500,000[23] from his music in 2010. In an interview for NPR's Planet Money, Alex Blumberg asks Coulton about the nature of his extraordinary success: "20 years ago, before the internet, before social media, would you be making a living as a musician?" Coulton's response: "Well, 20 years ago, I moved to New York City to make a living as a musician, and instead I got a software job. So the answer is no."[24]

Meanwhile, every time a big-name artist like Amanda Palmer or Ben Folds announces a crowdfunded project, there's a flurry of excitement, a temptation to speculate on The Future of Music in some broad sense, to extrapolate from a single story that something much bigger is happening. "People get excited about it, I suppose, because it's new and it's an opportunity — it's like maybe this is how music could come out and it could level the field," Ben Folds tells an interviewer: "Well, it's not going to. Let's say Kanye West decided to go do Kickstarter — he'd blow the Internet up. What good would that do? It wouldn't mean that the band next door is going to have a better chance."[25]

It's true: the one thing I know for certain about making music for a living — maybe the only thing anyone can ever know for certain about it — is that there's no easy way. The parameters and paradigms might indeed be shifting, and crowdfunding or something like it might well be the best way, if not the only way, for you to make the particular record that you feel you need to make. But there's danger in thinking that DIY is *the answer*, especially if you haven't properly defined the question. There are many questions and many answers and many complications.

In the case of crowdfunding, for instance, the celebrity factor hasn't been quite eliminated. It's a system that has a lot of potential for everybody, but it often works most spectacularly for those who are already established or well-known. Amanda Palmer's crowdfunded album may well be excellent, but she didn't raise upwards of $1 million just on the strength of a good idea — she already had a huge diehard fan base ready to get behind her and spread the word. For your average DIY artist it's still a slog — just a slog with a greater likelihood of a smaller reward.

It's also not universally true that any association with "the industry" will end in tears; this is not, nor can it ever really be, a black and white issue, a choice between being shackled and screwed or being gloriously free. "Being signed can be really good," Juju tells me:

> I think you're lucky if you come out unscathed and you're lucky if you make money and you're lucky if you get the record you want and you're lucky if you get on the radio and you're lucky if you get all the press and the festivals — you're probably also really talented, but you're pretty lucky. And all it takes is your A&R man to be sacked or leave the company for you to be screwed, you know. No one's gonna work your record. But I wouldn't have that nice guitar I'm playing if we hadn't been signed. Ben wouldn't have had the Hammond. I wouldn't have half the clothes I wear, quite frankly. And I wouldn't have been able to have some money and be relaxed for a little bit. So yeah — it can be great. It's just, like everything, there's always another side.

❧

There's something else, too. Although there seems to be a strong sense of community and camaraderie amongst the independent artists I've encountered, there's also a more abstract, slightly haunting sense of (albeit voluntary) isolation underpinning each effort. To adapt the old aphorism, with great freedom comes great responsibility. When I speak with self-described "gloom pop solo artist" Laura Kidd, who's just released her sophomore album as She Makes War, she tells me that it was a combination of principles and impatience that led her to release both of her albums independently. With the first album particularly, she says, "I didn't want anyone to have the right to say if it was good or not, because I knew it was what I wanted to make." Speaking about the implications of this kind of creative autonomy, though, she says: "Isn't it wonderful, that it's up to me? I can choose whatever I want to do. But because I can do whatever I want, because all the tools are there, and they're wonderful tools, sometimes there is a lot of pressure. Sometimes I don't quite know what do to."

That's the inevitable constraint of freedom, the curse of having control. The tyranny or weight of the blank page. If no one's jabbering on about hits and radio playlists, if you're really free to make whatever it is you want to make, how do you start it, let alone finish it? For one thing, you have to know what it is you want to make. You have to be certain of your idea, or certain enough to take the risk yourself. And you have to know how to create something you'll be independently proud of, regardless of how well or poorly received it is by others.

"I really want to do a record that I really like," Juju tells me when I ask her about the process of writing and recording Little Fish's second album. "With the first one, I think I achieved 50% of what I wanted to achieve [...] I think if you like what you do and nobody else likes it, that's fine. But if you do something that you don't really like, and not everybody really likes it, then you're pissed off." Kidd echoes this sentiment when she talks about her first album: "I knew it was what I wanted to make, so it was almost completely irrelevant if anyone thought it was good or not." And I realize that this kind of confidence, this kind of self-awareness and vision, is as crucial for artists (independent and otherwise) as having a strong community who are willing to put their money where their mouths are. It's as crucial as anything else, in fact. As Ben Folds says about his foray into crowdfunding: "We really are making it up as we go along"[26] – so I guess in the end all we can do is try to make something good.

VI. Home

This being the case, if I were asked to name the chief benefit of the house, I should say: the house shelters daydreaming, the house protects the dreamer, the house allows one to dream in peace. Thought and experience are not the only things that sanction human values. The values that belong to daydreaming mark humanity in its depths.

– Gaston Bachelard, *The Poetics of Space*

I first arrived in Oxford a few days after the city's favourite independent music venue closed its doors for good. The Zodiac was legendary; it had meant a lot to the Oxford music scene over the last decade, or so I'm told, functioning as a sort of home base for local bands and music fans. Its commercial takeover (by the Academy Music Group, who reopened it as the Carling Academy, later the O2 Academy) marked the end of an era – and I'd missed the whole thing.

I didn't even know I'd missed it. I didn't know about the Zodiac. I didn't know that Radiohead, whose music I had so often listened to as a teenager, were from Oxford, or that the catchy track *Alright*, which I'd heard often enough in my youth, had been written and performed by Oxford-based group Supergrass. As a newly-arrived, recently-graduated twenty-something with a penchant for costume dramas and libraries, I was preoccupied by the literary heritage of Oxford. Everything I knew about it I'd read in *Brideshead Revisited* or *Zuleika Dobson*. My understanding that the city had multiple and overlapping identities, many completely independent of the bookish thread I'd followed from California, developed very slowly, over a period of years. And it was only when I began to rewrite my mental map of the place to include my own haunts as well as those of Waugh's undergraduates or Beerbohm's femme fatale that I began to feel I could justly call it *home*.

Is it a coincidence, then, that this acceptance of Oxford as home – which included a resigned embrace of all that is ugly and humdrum about it – coincided with a period of heavy gig-going? Yes and no; I wouldn't say that my discovery of the music scene in Oxford significantly influenced my opinion of it as a place to live, but I would say that a necessary part of the process of making a home here included participating in the theatre of the gig. I would say that listening to live music helped me settle in.

When I started going to gigs here, it was usually to see bands who had been recommended by somebody I knew (or, indeed, whose members were people I knew) – so there was a kind of built-in sense of community, or at least amicability, from the get-go. I began to feel like I was part of something, even if it wasn't a very big thing, and even if I was only just on the periphery of it. I would run into people I hadn't planned to run into and we would go to the bar together and buy a beer and stand outside later chatting. I remember a particular evening in August – a gig in a little independent shop in east Oxford, part of the launch of Little Fish's debut album. I felt gratified that I knew not only two of the three band members, but their parents as well, who stood near me in the audience. Somehow, I thought, to know and be known by people's families was a significant thing. It validated me, made my presence here real.

I cycled home that evening in a summer storm – thunder, lightening, a giddy downpour, the cars slopping down the street, my bare legs washed clean by the rain. It was a quiet evening, my boyfriend away on a business trip. I made dinner for one, found an unopened bottle of wine in the kitchen and poured a glass. Before bed I brushed my teeth; I spat the foamy excess into the sink and thought, isn't it funny, that this is a sink in Oxford; that I have a sink in Oxford? It was good-funny; I experienced a pleasurable sensation of mild awe at my own surroundings – one of the final fizzes of amazement before the novelty would dissolve completely and the sink would forever be just a sink. Home. There's something almost disappointing about it, but something warm, too. I opened the window in my bedroom; it was silent outside – too late for the usual closing-time rabble, too early for the shrill students on their way home from some party or other. I read for a bit, from Bachelard's *The Poetics of Space*, which someone had recently lent me: "For our house is our corner of the world."

Of course, none of it had anything really to do with music, but when I remember that feeling, that period of transition, I remember it as being inextricably linked to that particular night, that gig, to the tap of feet and the bobbing of heads as the summer rain fell on familiar streets outside and familiar voices rang out inside.

Even so, even now, I'm an outsider here, as much by choice as by birth. There's an insularity about communities that I like to resist, for better or worse; even when I feel at home I love to play the visitor. I'm reminded of Geoff Dyer, writing about his return to England after a period of living abroad: "Back in the land where I belonged, back among my own tribe, I immediately missed not belonging, missed that strange home you can build out of homelessness, out of not belonging."[27]

For me, it's hard to separate the idea of belonging from the idea of a kind of partisanship – as if to belong in one place or group deprives you of your chance to belong in another simultaneously, as if some great choice must be made. I'm reminded of my more judgmental days, when I thought I could measure the social worth of someone based on his taste in music. If he liked what I deemed to be mainstream drivel I'd be scornful; if he liked what I professed to like, it meant maybe we could have a few beers and make out in his dorm room. (The irony here, of course, is that I spent two years in love with the boy who listened earnestly to Ashlee Simpson; the boy who introduced me to the Eels – infinitely cooler, in my dubious book – was barely a blip on the radar.) Because I saw the world in this black-and-white way, it made me wary of declaring my own allegiances: I wanted to be able to slip unnoticed between tribes, to wear whatever mask the situation required.

I'd like to think I'm above all that now, but my lingering insecurity was thrown into sharp relief recently when I discovered that people – complete strangers – were subscribing to a playlist I'd made on music streaming service Spotify. It was a playlist made up of songs I'd heard recently and liked and would soon grow bored of: not necessarily an accurate picture of my musical taste in general, if one could even create such a thing, but certainly an accurate picture of what I was spending a lot of time listening to that month. I hadn't realized that the playlist was publicly available, that anyone could see it and, worse, subscribe to it, which I can only assume implies a desire to listen to it.

I had the uneasy feeling of being watched. I found it difficult to add any further tracks to the playlist, even though it was my playlist, and it hardly mattered what anyone else thought of it. I was ambivalent about what these songs said about me – who, exactly, was this person who juxtaposed Lana Del Rey with Fleet Foxes and a cheesy country song she'd heard in an episode of *Friday Night Lights*, and did I like her, let alone want to be her? The thought that while I was debating this question someone I'd never met might be forming an opinion of me based on these somewhat arbitrary private choices was torturous.

I thought, then, of the private relationship with music: the way one's connection to certain songs is sometimes strengthened by the knowledge that no one else can observe this connection, read anything into it. Sometimes I can hear the neighbours' music coming through my study wall, and it occurred to me for the first time that the reverse was probably also true; every time I pressed repeat (sometimes, if a certain song was really helping me work, I'd listen to it as often as seven or eight times in a row) they, too, would be subjected to another performance. When I listened to Robert Johnson sing the blues, or the 90s pop songs I remembered growing up with, the sounds I heard – or scraps of them, at least – slipped into the cracks in the wall or out the open window, invading other people's spaces.

Somehow this knowledge disturbed and sobered me; it certainly seemed to change the tone of all those long solitary days spent at my desk. There's something about listening to music in the privacy of one's own home that seems sacred. I think of the word *shelter*, of what Bachelard writes: "the house shelters daydreaming, the house protects the dreamer." [28] But there is no perfect privacy, even in a private room. Even there, at home, at my desk, looking out at the overgrown garden and the cherry tree that this year had failed to produce any cherries, I could be overheard, observed, in a sense. I became aware, quite suddenly, that my desire to remain an outsider – in Oxford or anywhere – is really a desire to remain the judge, so as to avoid being judged. Distance shelters, too, and the outsider – the observer – can always claim that those inside don't understand him. The insider has no such protection, having been exposed.

The house seems to reverse this theory: *inside* the house one can sit safe and quiet, guarded by walls and doors. It's *outside*, where engagement with society is necessary, that poses a threat. To go outside, to leave the lonely house and enter the crowded world, is to risk rejection. So part of coming to terms with feeling at home somewhere is to come to terms, too, with feeling exposed, with feeling fragile as an individual yet strengthened by a sense of camaraderie. To an extent I find myself able to do that here because I can always, in an emergency, claim quite legitimately to be from elsewhere and therefore to belong elsewhere; I can always revert to feeling allegiance only to "that strange home you can build out of homelessness". But mostly I hover uncertainly on the door-step of acceptance: I say I see myself as an outsider, I say I want the perspective and objectivity that comes from being the observer, but I also say I'm at home here, and I mean it in some fairly deep sense; I feel I've earned it, just as I feel that the place itself has earned my affection.

The reason I mention all this is that when I think about music in Oxford (or anywhere, really), I think of the way music is part of the fabric of a place, the way the communities that form around music express their pride at having fostered local talent. Don't we love it when a superstar comes from our hometown? Don't we love to feel that we've been a part of something since before it even was something? There's a kind of musical patriotism that extends beyond the boundaries of music, and sometimes it's tricky to tell if you're justified in expressing that patriotism. Does the fact that I no longer feel amazed as I look down at my bland Oxford sink entitle me to feel I have some special connec-tion to the artists that also call this city home, or some ownership of their success? And if I do feel that way, does it mean that I must relin-quish my ties to elsewhere, to other things?

I don't know the answer to these questions. I do know that I like the feeling I get when I watch film-maker Jon Spira's 2009 documentary *Anyone Can Play Guitar*, which chronicles nearly 30 years of the Oxford music scene, from the late 1970s through 2007, when the Zodiac shut. When I watch it, I'm filled with pride, even if it's undeserved. *Look at what this place, my place, has produced!* I think. Whether the place chose me or I chose it is irrelevant; whether I had any hand in building the scene, whether I even witnessed any of it, whether I deserve to feel some bond to it, is all also irrelevant: for an hour or two I consider myself patrioti-cally and irrevocably *a part of it.*

I've seen the film a few times now, and I still find myself particularly moved by the story of The Candyskins, who kept teetering on the verge of major mainstream success before being yanked back from the edge as a result of things completely out of their control (a single called *Car Crash* was set to be released the week of Princess Diana's death, for instance). They were, like so many, victims of circumstance, bad timing.

Now I consider the possibility that in spite of politics or prejudices, where we're rooted has a very real impact on the way we listen to – and interact with – music. Sometimes I see ex-Candyskins guitarist Mark Cope having a drink in my local pub – his local pub too, I guess. He doesn't know me and I wouldn't know him if I hadn't seen the film; although The Candyskins did pretty well for themselves – their single

Monday Morning made it into the Top 40 of the UK Singles Chart, while another track featured on the soundtrack to a big Adam Sandler film – I'd never even heard of them until a few years ago. But there we are, sharing a space, at opposite ends of the same room, ordering pints from the same barman. And I find I want to own some of the Candyskins's disappointment, as I also want to own some of their considerable success, because to do so is to acknowledge an allegiance to this place – this pub, this street, this city.

❦

In July of 2011, a much-loved Oxford music magazine (the indomitable *Nightshift*, which is as integral a part of the music scene as the bands themselves) published fairly negative reviews of two recent releases by local artists. Ben, who happens to be friends with both of the reviewed artists, posted a response online, questioning the usefulness of such reviews:

> I get it. Ronan [Munro, editor of *Nightshift*] likes his music with a bit more bite. So do I, for the most part. I also get that Miriam [Jones] and Roger [Dalrymple] aren't cool. Neither am I. But I love listening to Miriam and Roger's music *because I know them*. I know them through the local music scene, and I know them as friends. When I think about it, all the music I've ever loved is by people I know, either as a friend or a fan.
>
> If Ronan had been there when Miriam played in my flat at the Little Fish house concert he would have got to know her. Her music may not be his favourite sort of music, but Miriam's difficult not to like in person. And once you understand where she's coming from the music makes a lot more sense.
>
> I don't want to be down on Ronan. He does a great job, and I'd be disappointed if I didn't disagree with him sometimes. It's more the whole idea of music reviews and the music press that I have trouble with. In real life people just don't engage with music by listening to a CD twice in a void and forming an opinion. People connect with the people behind the music. They take time to get to know them. It's partly a failing of the "CD and one-pager" press release format for albums. However well-written your press release

is, it won't be enough to get to know the people behind the music. All a critic can do with that is slot you into a particular category, pick two bands to compare you with and take the piss a bit.[29]

When I read Ben's post, I suddenly remembered a class I'd taken at university, as part of a degree in politics. It was called something ambiguous, like "Public Affairs", but ostensibly it was a class on spin: how to control conversations, how to present things in just the right way. Sometimes we would hold practice press conferences. We would field questions from our peers about a made-up thing – a fictional event or organization or political candidate. We would pause, where appropriate, to consider the important question: *what's the angle here?* Sometimes they call it narrative, story, but it's not deep like story. It's like attempting to capture story in a receptacle too shallow to contain it.

"When I think about it, all the music I've ever loved is by people I know, either as a friend or a fan," Ben writes. And that means something. These days a lot of what I listen to, too, is music that's been made by people I know (including both Ben and Miriam) – even if I know them only in the loosest sense of the word "know". And maybe that's because I'm lucky enough to know a number of talented people, but I think more likely it's because of the shared history we have, however tenuous it might be. The real story (not the angle, not the spin) is in the overlap between your life and their music. And sometimes that overlap is nothing more or less than a *place* – a dot on a map, a grubby old venue, a street. Shared geographies.

This wasn't something I really thought about before I moved to Oxford. Before I moved to Oxford I had sort of given up going to see live bands. I thought the whole thing was exhausting. It was exhausting to try to keep up with what was cool (though, in true hipster tradition, not too cool). It was exhausting to stand in big crowded rooms in Cambridge or Somerville, swaying next to all the girls with legwarmers and boys with striped polo shirts and sweatbands, so far away from the stage that I may as well have been back in my dorm room, with headphones on and the heating turned up. It was exhausting to see a band I really liked – Rilo Kiley, for instance, whose songs had cradled me through my first painful year away from home – and feel so detached. There I was, in darkness, rubbing sweaty shoulders with people I'd never met, watching Jenny Lewis strut around the stage in cowboy boots and tiny shorts, trying to feel something, but feeling nothing. The only real sensory memory I carry with me from that particular gig is of an intense envy of (or was it desire for?) Lewis's legs, which shone palely beneath the spotlight. As far as I was concerned, live music was the most sterile form of music, the surest way to feel distanced from a performer.

But then I moved to Oxford and started listening to people I knew (or sort of knew, or who knew people I knew) sing and play guitars and hit drums and stamp on loop pedals. And that changed things.

It didn't change my taste, not fundamentally. It didn't change my standards. I happen to like Miriam Jones's gentle voice and "tasteful and polished" country-twangy songs *anyway*. If I didn't know her and I heard her music somewhere – in the background of some emotional TV show scene, say, as a weary doctor strolls the corridors of the hospital or the football team jog out to the field – my attention would be captured; I'd want to know what the song was. Knowing a musician can't compensate for poor quality, but where good quality is a given, it can certainly augment the experience of listening. I guess what I'm saying is that there's music that you listen to and then there's music that you interact with, in whatever way happens to work for you: you interact with it emotionally, you contribute to or become part of its ongoing narrative, you situate yourself in it somehow.

And there's an aspect of that kind of interaction which is integrally linked to geography, to shared spaces – particularly where independent artists are concerned. As theatre-maker and academic Hannah Nicklin writes: "I think at the root of the ethics of DIY is something born of a place and community, and which offers a distinct alternative to the monoculture that thrives on top-down structures (the mainstream music industry e.g.) and 'one size fits all' models of entertainment. [...] DIY, in my opinion, is the best alternative there is, because it's grown and shaped by a certain place to fit and make room for the people that want to live in it."[30]

Of course, physical geography is now theoretically irrelevant to musicians, even DIY-ers. Communities that have no place in common can form easily and fluidly around music; the internet facilitates this, as does touring, to a certain extent.

When I speak to Manchester-based Little Fish fan Sophie Marfell, she talks fondly about how she and fellow Squid Frank Ralph "racked up quite a few miles between us, traveling to Little Fish gigs" last year. But even racking up miles is no longer necessary. If your goal as a fan is to help progress an artist's career, you can purchase his music or sing his praises to an audience of thousands without ever leaving your chair. If you want to interact with him, you can do that too – in fact a band with an active online presence might actually foster relationships that thrive on distance. The intimacy of a gig can, when necessary, be replaced by the intimacy of Twitter, so that a relationship with an album or an artist or another fan is possible no matter where you are.

So who needs common ground when there's common (cyber)space? In a sense, the band themselves become the common ground, functioning as the familiar streets and shops, the thing about which people can share knowledge. There they are, in Paris or Istanbul or Shanghai, still themselves, though "themselves" may well be an evolving thing. Anywhere in the world, they're the point on the map that you and I have in common, even if you and I have never set foot in the same city.

But even so – the significance of home remains. "Little Fish came home again," I wrote at the beginning of this book. To say this implies that they may have strayed from home; it also implies that they had a home to stray from in the first place. And they did stray, I think – or at least it seems that way retrospectively. When Juju talks about recording *Baffled and Beat* in Los Angeles, she speaks of "a difference between American and English rock". It "didn't work for us," she says. "The culture didn't work ... which I think is why the music got a bit lost." Ultimately, she tells me, "had I known what I know now [...] I wouldn't have made the record in America."

It's tempting to read regret into that statement, to construe making the album in America as a mistake, but I think there's something else, too – a sense that if Little Fish hadn't made that record in America, Juju wouldn't be so certain that the next one should be made in Britain. Sometimes it takes leaving your home to recognize that you had one in the first place.

❦

These days, Ben and Juju live in a bungalow on the outskirts of the city. Oxford isn't big, but it takes me almost an hour to cycle there, especially if there's a strong headwind or I've forgotten to pump my tires – so it feels quite remote, like it inhabits its own unique corner of the universe. It's quiet and residential; the area reminds me a little of America, of aimless drives with a college boyfriend who lived in a suburb of Boston. There are wide tree-lined roads, homes set off from the street. The house itself is tidy and warm, with a big lawn, meticulously mowed, and lines of potted plants out front – an ambitious array of roses and tomatoes and herbs, plants that look remarkably well-tended and healthy.

Is this how I imagined musicians lived? I suppose the truth is I never thought much about the rock star at home, though I remember vividly the tasteless opulence on display in MTV's Cribs – the California palaces of pop-punk guitarists, rappers' garages stuffed to the gills with cars. But the musician – regardless of the extent of his financial or commercial success – is only human: he needs a home, a place to rest his head, a refuge or a base.

For Ben and Juju, the home – this home in particular, this funny bungalow – is also the backdrop to their new album. The line between their lives as people and their lives as musicians has always been blurred, if it's existed at all (case in point: their happy coexistence as both band mates and lovers; neither relationship ever seems more dominant than the other). But now they've literally brought the whole operation home, and it's a brave move: there's nowhere left to hide, no escape, no way to walk away at the end of the day.

One summer afternoon I visit them at the bungalow. I'm a little early, and Juju is finishing the laundry. I help her fold big sheets, put pillows in clean cases. I've been here before, for social reasons, for dinner or tea, to sit and talk. This was where they told me, earlier in the year, the roads still lined with frost and the sky already dark around the edges at three or four o'clock, that they were expecting a baby. It seemed then like a domestic sanctuary, a place untroubled by the struggles and uncertainty of being a musician; it was where they were going to raise their child, a task fraught with its own particular kind of struggle and uncertainty. Now, though, I consider its function as a site for the creation of music. It's where Juju writes, where she and Ben practice and tweak and explore the nuances of their sound. It's where their new sound was born, in a way, and where the evolution from three-piece rock band to whatever comes next will be documented; they're hard at work on the second album now, playing in the garage, banging pots and pans together, making noise with whatever's in reach.

Juju mentions the garage often in our interviews. It seems important to her to stress how local, how scrappy and resourceful, they've become as a band. "I want to make do with what we've got, but the real way," she says. "I don't want to be in a Dave Grohl garage. I bet his garage is nothing like our garage. No, we're recording in a *garage*." As we sit outside in the warm dusk, watching birds, peeling oranges, she says: "My

94

philosophy with this record is just to do as much of it as we can ourselves, and don't ask for anything, because then you don't owe anybody
anything. Which is why we're doing it in our garage and we've only got
two mics and no cymbals. It's fine. We've got pots and pans."

She tells me the reasons for this approach are twofold: "One, yes, I
want to do it, and two, I also have to do it. Because there is no other
way." She thinks the sound they'll get by playing in their garage is a more
honest sound, truer to who they are as a band, than the one they got
recording in a shiny LA studio four years ago – and, as an independent
artist with no recourse to the cash required to hire expensive studios and
producers, it's just as well that she feels this way.

But I wonder if it's not just this combination of preference and
necessity that led Little Fish down the DIY road and into their garage.
I wonder if it's also a way of making the place home, marking the
territory, letting the territory mark them. The record will forever be
linked to this place, even if they move next month or next year. The place
will forever be linked to the record. It's a record of the place, in a sense:
a record not just of the place in their lives that they're in – Juju heavily
pregnant, this as-yet-unnamed record just a promise, a series of rough
cuts and ideas – but also of the home they're building, have built.

What does sound have to do with the place it's created? On the one
hand, nothing, really – unless you're at a live gig, I suppose, where
things like acoustics (and, perhaps, the colour of the wallpaper – to
which, writes Alain de Botton, "we are inconveniently vulnerable"[31])
make a measurable difference to the quality of the sound and the experience of taking it in. Who knows where Little Fish fans will be when they
hear the band's second record; who knows what their surroundings will
look like, what their mood will be? You can't easily hear a mowed lawn,
a warm fire, a garage crowded with makeshift musical instruments. And
yet there's a sense in which you can, a sense in which these things are
implicit. They're an irrevocable part of the story – not just the story of
the record, but the story of the band, of the people who made the
record, who make the music now, on stage in front of you, humming
and strumming and pounding away.

Conclusion

The book has ended, but I'm still stuck on that question, the one I posed at the start, the one that sparked this whole project: "*Why do it?*" I mean when the odds are so against you, when the money has stopped coming in (or, more likely, never came in at all), when the room is empty and a string snaps or a voice cracks, when you know damn well that you ought to pack it all in: why keep going? I think of the question that Juju asks herself when she sings – or, rather, howls – the eponymous song: *am I crazy?* And I think, well, probably, yes.

"*Why do it?*" is certainly not a question confined to music, though music makes a particularly good backdrop against which to explore it. Musicians inhabit an absurd world: loud, crowded, endlessly frustrating. And sometimes it seems that everyone I meet is a musician. The two men I share a table with at the pub one busy evening are, of course, in a band. The writer of books and poems is, of course, also a writer of songs. The childhood friend I haven't seen for years is, it turns out, a drummer, going on tour next month. The bartender, the entrepreneur, the farmer: all musicians also. I like this ubiquitousness; it hints at the appealingly classless nature of musicianship, particularly independent musicianship. All of these people I meet have in common certain struggles and certain passions and a certain vocabulary, whether they play for hobby or livelihood.

There's another good argument for writing about music now, too. Advances in technology, shifting attitudes towards what has been historically an overbearing industry, and a growing awareness of alternative approaches to recording and distributing music, have combined to generate a particularly interesting – if volatile – climate. It's impossible to look at "music" – as a business, a form of entertainment, a way of life – and not perceive that something significant either is happening or might happen soon. Analogous things are happening or might happen soon in other industries, too – including the publishing industry, as the existence of this very book is testament to. And when the old model or the old world is no longer the only model or the only world – when the rock'n'roll myth is exposed as just that, a myth – it's somehow easier to break apart the whole messy thing and examine it in greater, stranger depth.

But writing about something *as it's happening* – like writing about music made by living people as opposed to dead people – has its own particular set of complications. I've often had the sense, whilst working on this book, and particularly whilst trying to finish it, that I'm sitting much too close to an impressionist painting, or that I've thoroughly dissected something but forgotten, in the process, what the purpose of dissecting it was, and now I'm left facing a table covered with unidentifiable innards. Only the passage of time can provide the distance I would need for a different kind of perspective; it may be that in a few years the issues about music and survival that Little Fish and I have found so pressing resolve themselves organically – or indeed that we're still asking the same questions, just as urgently, in two hundred years.

On the subject of time, and change, and the impossibility of knowing, I want to also acknowledge a more sombre aspect of this project. A few months ago, I ran into an old friend of Juju's, who's known the band since the beginning. When I told him about the book, he suggested that in a sense I was writing a eulogy. At the time I thought the word was too strong, or at least carried too many negative connotations. But the truth is I don't disagree: this is a eulogy, for the Old Little Fish, for what (and who) they once were – a way of marking all that they accomplished in that incarnation but drawing a firm line between Then and Now. I didn't know Little Fish Then, so it's relatively easy for me to allude to their past without sentimentality. I realize it may not be so easy for them to read about it, or for you to, who may know that part of their history much more intimately.

At the same time, though, this book is primarily a hopeful document – not predicting the future, but certainly imagining that a future is possible, and will continue to be possible, indefinitely, as long as there's a will to write and sing.

As far as the band itself is concerned, as far as the specifics of that future – well, it won't come as a surprise to anyone that I don't know what will happen to Little Fish. Ben and Juju have just finished writing the second album; I heard a few tracks at the beginning, very rough versions, pumped out through car stereo speakers. They sounded different to anything else I've ever heard Little Fish play, which makes sense. I sat in their manager's office while Juju played him one track that she was unsure about. His face was rigid, as she'd promised me it would be: whatever he felt about it, emotionally or professionally, he did not reveal there, not with his eyes or in his brief, non-committal comments afterward.

Meanwhile I sat still and smiled and tapped my toes against the floor. I could imagine hearing this song on the radio, on the dance floor, somewhere, anywhere. But the gap between imagining something and realizing it is huge, sometimes irreconcilably so, and anyway I have no doubt that the next time I hear any of the new songs – played live, or on my laptop, as part of a fully-fledged album – they'll sound at least a little different. The important thing for now is that Juju is excited when she talks about the record, which they plan to release in early 2013, and about music in general, regardless of – or perhaps because of – how little she can predict about the future.

In the meantime, Ben and Juju have been waiting for a baby to arrive. I wasn't necessarily going to write about this, but today, just this morning, I received an email from them. Attached was a black-and-white photo of Ben holding their son, whose eyes are closed, whose head is covered by one of those funny white hospital caps. When I started, I had no way of imagining that this would be the conclusion to the particular little piece of the Little Fish story that I've had the pleasure of documenting, but in many ways I can't imagine anything more appropriate or poetic, and it has to be acknowledged. New life, the end of an era, a whole new set of financial concerns and constraints, all of that. And a break from playing and recording.

Physically that break is necessary, particularly for Juju. But perhaps it's also emotionally convenient. A hiatus, a chance to regroup, gather strength. "Can't wait until next year when we can rise like toast from the toaster with a new album, new line-up, new book and new baby," Juju captioned a photograph of herself, full-term, white t-shirt and black leather jacket lifted to reveal the swell of her belly. I like the lightheartedness and the domesticity of the phrase "rise like toast from the toaster" – the way it hints at the fact that Juju is neither as serious or as self-assured as you might be tempted to think, the way it belies an insecurity whilst simultaneously promising something, even if you're not sure what. But also, I think, I've been thinking about this too much now: I'm reading into things that don't need reading into. I want to laugh at the turn of phrase and enjoy the fact that my friends have a tiny son with tiny hands and tiny feet.

So a pause. Ben's taken on a full-time job, one that perfectly utilizes his skills and interests. He seems happy. I want to be happy for him, and I am, but I also feel a little defeated, if I think about it for too long. Like, we tried, and we kind of failed. But failed at what, exactly? Did we ever really believe that we could build and then inhabit a world where everything went exactly as we wanted it to — where we attained just the right amount of success, just the right amount of income, just the right amount of freedom? I guess at the bottom of my heart I didn't really; I'm too much a pessimist. But I wanted to try anyhow. I wanted us all to try, at least to have the opportunity to try. To learn what was important, to learn what we could not sacrifice and what we could.

I've just finished a trial shift as a waitress at a restaurant. Not that I'm going to make a career as a waitress. Not that I even necessarily could; I'm not great at multi-tasking, or balancing delicate things on trays, for that matter. Just that I thought maybe it was time to swallow my pride, at least for an afternoon. Just that I've been self-employed for almost exactly a year, and I've learned that although things usually work out, often in ways you couldn't possibly expect, it's tiring to not know how they'll work out, and I'm tired of being so tired all the time. So, yes, we tried, and we kind of failed, if this was an experiment that can be measured so easily; if it was an experiment at all. I think I can finally admit that, and not feel that I've reneged on some unspoken promise to Fight The Man.

But then again, in a sense the admittance of defeat is a victory in itself: once it isn't about winning and losing, make or break, my way or the highway, it's just about doing whatever it is you're doing, from one moment to the next, and that's okay. That's the way it should be. The questions are endless: *Will Little Fish's next record sell millions of copies? Will they sign to a label again? Will they be part of a movement of independent artists who are able to support themselves thanks to a strong group of fans and the magic of the internet? Will their third album sound completely different to their second, which sounds completely different to their first? Will they decide to give it all up and start their own apple juice company instead?* But it seems easier to face them when there's no pressure to prove that one thing or another is best, when there's no pressure to do anything except, as Juju puts it, make a record you actually like. The trick is to put yourself in a place where you can feel, even if briefly, that lack of pressure. You'll have to improvise: maybe it takes a calculated effort – harnessing the power of the internet, the power of fans, the power of sheer persistence. Maybe it takes lying to yourself, or buying into a dangerous myth, or maxing out your credit cards and busking for cash, or telling yourself that nothing else matters. Maybe it takes having another, concurrent career – "a double life", as Paul Auster calls it.[32] But the moral of this story is: whatever it takes, get there, to that place.

I'm reminded of what Juju says when I ask her what keeps her afloat if she's having a rough time: "swimming". Then she laughs, and it's almost a joke, or ostensibly a joke, but also not at all a joke. I think of the soothing view of the pool floor, the roll of the head and the intake of breath, the steady exhalation underwater. To breathe like that, to glide like that, is a miraculous thing. Each lap is isolated in time: however many seconds of complete concentration and complete mindlessness. Just floating, making slow happy progress. Outside, a man walks the length of the pool much faster and with much less effort, but never mind him.

That's the inner drive; that's the place to get to.

This morning, looking at the photo they've sent, I wonder if Ben and Juju's child will be a musician. I can't help it: it's such an obvious route for the imagination to take. I suppose everyone thinks like that about their friends' children, about their own children. And I consider the possibility that everything Ben and Juju do from here on out will be for him, not for themselves. I still suffer from the selfishness of extreme youth (measured not only in years but in lack of experience: still childless, unmarried, unfettered), but I can appreciate pretty innately the way it changes things to have a dependent. For the first time I consider the possibility that's always been there, the one thing I should always have seen: that what we do, what we discover or don't discover, the books and songs we write, won't benefit us but him. And maybe he'll be the real trailblazer, the revolutionary, the guitarist who's got it all figured out. Or maybe he'll eschew his parents' occupation entirely. He'll be an investment banker or an astrophysicist or a sommelier or a grocer.

We can't know. We can never know. We can just keep playing and keep guessing.

Interviews

A book about music is really a book about people. Analysis is useful; commentary on The State of The Music Industry or The Future of Music or How To Make a Living Making Music is useful. But none of it would matter if it wasn't for the musicians and the fans and everyone in between. As Christopher Small writes: "This book, then, is not so much about music as it is about people, about people as they play and sing, as they listen and compose."[33]

I know these are just roles we play. The musician, the composer, the performer, the listener: she's always also someone else. As important a part of her identity as the music may be, it's never all of it. (Juju acknowledges this in an interview: "music is important to me, and I really enjoy it when I'm doing it," she says, "but it's not *everything* that I enjoy.") But the inverse is not true: music is nothing without people. It has no life without us.

Conducting interviews, therefore, was a fairly large part of the process of writing this book. I wanted to get different perspectives, to talk to people with disparate histories, roles, and ideas. I spoke with musicians, mainly, but others, too, and these people have all lent their voices to the book; they give it a depth and an emotional resonance it would otherwise lack. Their stories and their particular viewpoints are not just what make the analysis matter, but also what makes it possible in the first place. It's one thing to write about the collective experience, the ground common to everyone who has a relationship with music – but the experience of the individual, the more local experience, is what allows us to glimpse the bigger picture.

Largely for this reason, transcripts of a few selected interviews follow. There's Juju, of course, whose voice is the heart of Little Fish. And there's Ben, speaking not just as a member of Little Fish but as a songwriter and performer in his own right, a self-described geek, and, most recently, an employee of online music platform Bandcamp. Both are important perspectives to feature in a book that uses the ongoing journey of Little Fish as its central narrative.

The other three interviews are somewhat more tangential, but each is representative of important attitudes towards music, and complements the rest of the text particularly well. The first interviewee, Laura Kidd, is an independent musician. She's a bit of an outsider, a wild card in this book – not Oxford-based, not connected to Little Fish except socially (I first met her after she played a house concert in Ben's flat). Originally I'd intended to use her interview for background research, for sound bites, but when I looked over the transcribed conversation I found that she had articulated a number of points central to the book, and it's valuable to see these ideas in situ – that is, as applied by actual musicians in real situations, rather than described theoretically.

Laura's interview is followed by one with Gaz Coombes. Gaz was the lead vocalist and guitarist for Supergrass, one of the best-known bands to come out of the Oxford music scene. Over a 17-year long career, Supergrass released six studio albums, each one entering the top 20. After the band split in 2010, Gaz continued his career as a producer and musician, and his debut solo album, *Here Come the Bombs*, was released in May 2012. He has worked with Little Fish (including to produce their single *Wonderful*) and known them for a number of years, so I was interested in his thoughts on their evolution as a band as well as his more general views on the business of making music, particularly from the perspective of someone who's enjoyed a long and quite successful career.

I've also featured an interview with Robert Rosenberg of Trinifold Management. Robert manages Little Fish, but Trinifold have also managed acts including The Who, Robert Plant, and Judas Priest. Of everyone I interviewed, Robert belongs most firmly in the "old school industry" camp, though his willingness to work with a band like Little Fish speaks positively to his relative open-mindedness. But this strong connection to the traditional, capital-i Industry (the "huge empire", to borrow Louis Barabbas's phrase) is precisely why I want to highlight Robert's point of view.

LAURA KIDD

Laura Kidd is a multi-instrumentalist, visual artist, blogger, and videographer. As a bassist and singer, she's toured the world with acts including Tricky, A-Ha, The Penelopes, I Blame Coco, The Young Punx, and Alex Parks. Under the umbrella of her solo project, She Makes War, Laura has released two albums: the debut Disarm in September 2010, followed by Little Battles in April 2012. She has written and spoken extensively about DIY and the independent musician. I've known Laura for a few years, as both a musician and a friend, and was pleased to be able to get her perspective on some of the issues addressed in this book. The following is an edited version of a conversation conducted with Laura via Skype in May of 2012.

Miranda Ward: How did you start out as a musician?

Laura Kidd: I started playing music when I was really little. I was taught to read music and encouraged to do all that stuff when I was like five years old. And then when I was about 15, I'd been playing guitar a little bit... and I had this moment where I was like, "I'm going to be a singer". I didn't know how, really, or what it entailed, but in my head I was like, I'm gonna start an indie band, because that just seemed like the thing I was gonna do. So I started a band with these boys from school. And that was my first experience of gigging and stuff. I moved to London because I wanted to join a band, and I was in various bands, and then the session thing kind of gradually happened.

I think it was 2004 when She Makes War started. But it started as a three-piece band. ... I was introduced to a drummer by these guys who wanted to manage this band ... but me and the drummer weren't getting on with the view these managers had for us, and I decided it should be just our thing. Then the drummer left. So I went solo in 2005, without having ever released anything. And from then it was a gradual process of refining my sound, figuring out what I wanted to write. It took quite a while. I was busy, you know, I had a freelance career, session music, video-making. But in the meantime, I was on Twitter, and using social media, just out of interest, not to try and sell stuff, and that's been a big thing.

MW: **Is there any particular reason that you decided you wanted to be independent and do all this stuff yourself – was it based on principles, or because you think it works out better for the artist, or something else?**

LK: It started out as a principle thing. It's not like I've been offered lots of major label deals and I've gone "no". But I also haven't looked for them. So with the first album, I made it in solitude – even the creative process was very enclosed. And that was because I wanted to make a thing without any outside influence at all – whether that would have been a label, a manager, whoever. My co-producer Myles [Clarke] is really wonderful at letting me do what I want to do. He obviously added lots of stuff, technical, engineering – but he didn't say anything about what I should or shouldn't do, which I so appreciate, because that's definitely what I needed at the time – just to make the thing I needed to make and see if it worked. And for me it did, because I was really proud of it. And then I made the definite decision not to try and shop it around to anyone, because I didn't want to feel like I was in a position of asking permission. I didn't want anyone to have the right to say if it was good or not, because I knew it was what I wanted to make, so it was almost completely irrelevant if anyone thought it was good or not. So that was definitely on purpose.

With the second album, what I thought I might do is make it, and then get someone on board to help me get it out into the world, whether that was a label or a manager or whoever. But then I got too impatient. I just wanted to put it out. So yeah. I think along the way I've realized what I can do is sort of demonstrate to others that there are no excuses. And yes, I do happen to work as a video-maker. I've been doing that for quite a long time. So yes, it's easier for me to get a video made on the cheap or whatever or with various friends. But I still believe that every-one could do that.

MW: **And lots of people have other skills like that that are transfera-ble. If you're a web developer, you can build your own website, and so on. You have to be a jack of all trades, in a sense.**

LK: Yeah, and I think people get caught up in this idea that everything else becomes more important than the music, but it's your choice. I choose that the other parts of what I do are an interesting creative output for me as well. So I made my own website because, well, for one thing it doesn't cost me anything but time, because there is a money issue, because I don't have any funding other than what I make doing work. So that's part of it, but it's also because I feel like that's creative too, making a website that I like. Not everyone's like me; I'm not saying that everyone should make their own website. But you can definitely find someone who will do it for you. I just feel like artists should have input into everything that's representing them, whether that's a video, a photo shoot, website, anything – why would you not want to be involved?

MW: **What does success mean to you – both personally and as a musi-cian? What would make you feel like you'd been successful?**

LK: I love that you're asking this, because I always say to people that they need to define their own success, otherwise they'll never know if they've got it or not. Success for me is finishing a song, and listening to it, and thinking, yes, that sounds like how it sounds in my head. And it's conveying the emotion that I want it to convey. And I'm not pretending that I don't want anyone to listen to it. I really love that people listen to it, and people send me comments and stuff. But what I'm very careful to keep in my mind is that it doesn't matter how many times someone writes, "that song's amazing, you're amazing" or whatever – that's nice, and it's flattering. But if someone calls me amazing, or if someone calls me utterly shit, neither of those things makes the slightest difference to how I feel about my music. So that's really important to me. And the reason for that is that I definitely only put stuff out or share stuff that I'm com-pletely happy with, happy that I've made it the way I wanted to make it, if that makes sense. So I don't feel judged, negatively or positively. The only time I get pissed off is when journalists make horrible factual errors, or lazy comparisons.

MW: It's interesting what you say about the sense of completion that you feel when you write a song. For you, is making good music an end in itself, or a means to an end?

LK: It's an end in itself. I don't think that music is a means to an end, because that sort of implies that the end would be, you know, I don't know, adulation or a great big shiny house.

MW: Which it definitely is for some people, I think.

LK: Oh yeah, totally. But I think – I genuinely have an issue with the idea of luxury in our world. I don't support the idea that people should make vast amounts of money from something when other people don't have food and water and shelter. That's a very socialist approach probably. Anyway, I have a major issue with that in general – it's nothing to do with music specifically. So I would not ever want to be in a position where I'm earning vast amounts of money and then buying a shiny house and lording it over other people. I think that's odd.

I think of music, and playing music, as dating back to the times when people would go to village to village, you know, sharing music and being given food and board – troubadouring, I guess. That's why I like playing tiny weird shows, and staying in people's houses instead of staying in hotels. It's not really just that I don't have any money, although that's part of it. It's because it's a more meaningful experience. So even touring – touring's not a means to an end for me either, touring is the end, touring is the life. I want to live an artistic, musical life, and the end of the journey is not important. So, music not being a means to an end: for me, it's the fabric of my life, and yes of course, I need to make some money, and I need to pay rent and all that sort of stuff. But I'm quite happy to do that through other means, so that the pressure isn't on my music to make that money.

But I have reached a point where it's very difficult to spend as much time as I want and need to spend on the She Makes War project without things getting compromised. So I want to do more of my music and less of the things that make money, which means it's getting to be an interesting time. What I've recently started dabbling in, which I've never done before, is merchandise. So I've made t-shirts for the first time, and started selling postcard packs, and planning out different releases – partly with a view to there being some money coming in from it. I suppose I have the idea that at least everything should cover its own cost.

And then I don't have to make a lot of money in my other jobs to keep going.

But then there's this whole thorny issue, like if I'm playing a gig: am I playing a gig to advertise a t-shirt, or to advertise an album that someone might want to buy, or am I playing a gig because I'm playing a gig? And so – I mean, I obviously think that is the important part. It's lovely if people buy CDs after, and I have to get over this slight uncomfortable feeling I have of saying, "I've got CDs for sale" during a set – I hate doing that.

MW: I was reading something about that – it was a case study about a band who had spent months playing gigs and plugging their CD a couple times throughout the gig, and they were selling a decent number of CDs. And then they changed their tactic and started saying, look, we really want to share this CD with you – please don't leave without one. Pay whatever you can, if you can, or don't pay for it if you can't. And they drastically increased their sales.[34]

LK: That's really nice. My friends Hope and Social do that – they have this pay-what-you-want thing, online and also at gigs. And they also explain how much the production is, to release a CD. And a lot of people do that online now.

The only thing with that is that I get myself in a bit of a muddle sometimes over prices. I feel a bit bad if I sell a CD online and people are paying five quid for it or something, but then they find out later they could have had it for three quid at a gig – that's the only problem for me, is this discrepancy, and trying to keep everything fair. With the new album, I did a PledgeMusic campaign, which covered some of the costs of making it. (It also cost a lot to produce the things that were the incentives, but that's a whole other blog post I can write!) So the reason that *Little Battles* started as £3 minimum on Bandcamp just for a download is because everybody who supported on PledgeMusic it had to pay eight quid. But then that muddled the whole thing because I really truly support the pay what you think it's worth [PWYTIW] model – I think it's really good, and it also reminds musicians that your music's only worth what it's worth to the listener. I mean the worth to you should remain the same whether they like it or not, like I was saying before. But the financial worth to the listener – it's up to them. So I decided to make it PWYTIW to bring it in line with most of my other releases.

MW: I think in the case of your PledgeMusic campaign, at least for me, I felt like I was not just paying for the thing, the album itself – I was also paying to be part of that initial process. I was paying to help make it possible. It's the same thing with the book that I'm writing – you know, people have already paid money, and the book isn't even going to be out until much later in the year. And yes, if there's a trade edition it will be somewhat cheaper than that special edition hardback was. But I think the reason people spend money on crowd-funded projects, whether that's through Kickstarter or PledgeMusic or Unbound or whatever, is for the privilege and satisfaction of helping make something happen. That's what you're paying more for. You're not paying more for the exact same thing – you're getting a totally different experience, and you have a different relationship to that product, I think, in the end.

LK: That's a really good point. So it's an issue that's ongoing, and it's something I can change, at any point. And that's something – isn't it wonderful, that it's up to me, I can choose whatever I want to do. But because we can do whatever we want, because all the tools are there, and they're wonderful tools, sometimes there is a lot of pressure. Sometimes I don't quite know what to do – I could do anything. Because I can make videos, I can do Photoshop and whatever, it means I could do anything at any point. There are no limits. And it's hard to be disciplined about it. I read this brilliant blog post recently, and it was all about how too many ideas can just kill your energy for the stuff you have to get done. Because I could have a new idea and just spend all my time planning it. But then I still have to do the stuff I was gonna do before, which is more impor-tant. So I now have an ideas list. Otherwise you just get nothing done, do you?

MW: I want to talk just a little bit about your feelings about "the music industry". I get the impression sometimes that there's a sense that the music world is black and white, and you're either independ-ent or you've sold out, and you either do everything yourself, or you're a puppet. Do you feel like that characterization is valid?

LK: Well, I think there are so many shades of grey now, which is wonderful. I think that there were always people making great music that are nothing to do with, inverted commas, "the music industry", and that's only grown and gotten better since all the tools have come

along to make it easier for DIY. I think there is a problem at the moment
– it's almost like there's this worthiness about being DIY, and then the
next step is that you're not anymore. And I think that's very shortsighted.
From my perspective, I'm a DIY artist. I do everything myself, I have no
team, I have no manager, I have nothing else at all. I have some friends
who help me out sometimes, but they're really busy, and so it's really
hard, and mainly it's just me, staying up until the middle of the night,
doing Wordpress. Which is fine. But as I said before, what I'm trying to
do is more music, less work work, like paid work. Which means that it
has to – something has to give. Because I just can't continue the way I
am. It's exhausting. Wonderful, but exhausting. So I'm trying to figure
out what the next stage of DIY is, and I'm talking to a few friends,
musician friends and other people about it. And we really need to define
the language for that, so that people know what we're talking about –
like, what could the next sort of version of the team be? So someone like
Amanda Palmer – there are so many things she does brilliantly, whether
you like her music or not – and she's interesting, because she has a
proper team, because she obviously has revenue coming in to be able to
pay these people. And that's quite a nice example, something to strive
for.

MW: I guess the thing is, when you can raise, with a snap of your
fingers, a hundred thousand dollars on Kickstarter, you can pay a team,
can't you. You've got that power then.

LK: Definitely. She's doing things on a major record label scale, you
know. She was trying to raise a hundred thousand dollars, wasn't she,
but she's raised much more. A hundred thousand dollars is such a lot of
money. You don't need that much money to put a record out at all. So
the scale she's talking about is interesting, because it's kind of compara-
ble to the PR budget for at least a big indie label. It's all very interesting.
What I've always tried to do with my project is make it so the music is
of a quality, and the production and the artwork and everything is of a
quality, that would rival a major indie label. Not because I'm trying to
compete, but because I want my stuff to be of that quality.

So by the same token, I'd quite like to use some of the bits of "the
music industry" to help with that. I have used a PR company for the
latest album – with mixed results, which is a whole other conversation.
Because I am trying to be in that world, on my own terms. That comes
with all sorts of negative aspects – like, okay, so, I use this name My Big

Sister for my recordings now. The reason I'm doing that is because I'm starting a collective, a musicians' collective, which is going to have a blog and podcasts and events. And I didn't think about it in terms of, "I'm gonna pretend I've got a label so that people take me more seriously!" That didn't cross my mind. But then I got into Q magazine, and I think it's because it looks like I've got a label. And they talked about how my first album was self-released, and now this one's a step up. Which is hilarious, because nothing's changed! But the thing is – one, that I'm even in the magazine at all, and two, they felt they could slag it off much more freely, because it's on a label. The distance that gave them from me meant that they ripped into it.

So yes, it's a whole thorny thing. I think people have to find their own way; they need to decide, like you were saying before, what their own success is. Define your success. What are you trying to do? Is your music a means to an end? For me it's not – the music is the thing, and everything else is the thing, touring is the thing. It's not what might happen if I tour or anything like that. But I think that's an unhealthy way to look at anything, if you think about it. If you think, "oh, I'm gonna win the lottery one day, so all this is just passing time until then" – that's completely pointless. And having a big success like Rihanna or someone like that, those sort of massive smash hits, that's lottery-winning statistics. And that's the problem with, again in inverted commas, "the music industry", or "the record business" – because that's just a blip in terms of how long the universe and humans have been around, it's a tiny blip, of music as product, music as a shiny, sexualized, plastic product.

MW: **Right – it's built on a story, which has happened for a very small group of musicians, where you get rich quick. And that's great, but it can't sustain everybody else.**

LK: Yeah, and it's been perpetuated by TV shows like *Cribs*, and whatever, all the adverts saying "you should have this shiny thing!"

MW: **Yeah, I remember watching MTV when it became all about, not about the music, but basically about what you could buy if you were famous.**

LK: And it doesn't matter how brilliant you are – especially as a woman. It doesn't matter how brilliant your voice is, or how great the songs are that you've had written for you or whatever, you still have to take your clothes off, don't you? Beyoncé has the most amazing voice, and she still has to wiggle her arse around. What the fuck is going on there? It's like there are two separate things – there's music as shiny sex product, and there's music as an expression of your innermost emotions. Now I'm not saying that there isn't any crossover – because maybe someone's expressing their emotions *and* taking their top off. I mean Amanda Palmer, again, great example: she takes pictures of herself with her top off and whatever. But the difference is, she's not portraying herself as being sexually available to entice people to buy her record. She totally owns it. And I choose not to be too – I choose not to do anything like that.

MW: **So I think there are a few ways, when you're creating something, that you can think about how commercially viable it is. You can think about it as you're writing your songs. You can think, as part of the writing process: "will this be a hit, will it get played on Radio 1?" And you can also think about how you present yourself. You can think, "am I gonna look sexy to people when they see me, and is that gonna help me sell more stuff?"**

LK: [Laughs] I must admit, neither of those things ever cross my mind, ever. And I'm really glad. That's why I'm laughing – you're not wrong, a lot of people who are much more successful than me probably do think, "hmm, should I do this, will it make people buy things?" Maybe I should sometimes think that. But mostly I'm just thinking, "*hmm, what animal shall I dress up as today?*" Because I try to tell stories. I want to make something really magical, and so that's – you know, again, all of this could look really fey and contrived, like, "oh, she dresses as a unicorn, what a dick". But I just want things to be a bit weird and magical.

GAZ COOMBES

Gaz Coombes was the lead vocalist and guitarist for Supergrass until the band's split in 2010. I spoke to him at his home in January 2012, a few months before the release of his first solo album, Here Come the Bombs.

Miranda Ward: So one of the things that I'm looking at is what happens when change occurs in a musical career, whether it's that your drummer leaves your band or that you decide to go in a completely different direction. And I know that for you, doing this solo thing is a real departure from what you've spent the last fifteen years doing. Is it that you're now doing something that's more personal? What's the motivation?

Gaz Coombes: In the band, each of the individual characters has their way and their approach and their influences, and I think in an ideal situation, when you've got a band that's really kind of firing, all of those things work together and really complement each other. And I think that's the great thing about a band when it happens. But when the band finished, I felt that I could really explore what I'd done in early writing stages and early demo stages to a larger degree. I think in a way I sort of felt that I hadn't found my voice, sort of personally really. I think we had a collective voice, and that's really kind of killer when it works, when it connects, which is what we did for quite a few years. And I'm happy about that. I don't regret not finding my personal voice earlier on – I think because otherwise Supergrass wouldn't have been as it was. But it's just a case of sort of like fuck, actually man, what would I sound like if I were to do a record, who would it be? I think that was just a really exciting creative prospect.

And also...I suppose that one consistent through my life is trying to rise to the challenges that come along. There have been a few positives and negatives, but you just always try and rise to it and see if you can get past it, get through it. And this was another one. It's kind of like look, you know, I know that there's loads of delegation that goes on in bands and I know in the studio we'd often sort of share that load, so it wasn't too stressful for anyone, but we'd all have our moments, you know, taking charge in a way. But to do it all – I was sort of just interested to see if I was capable. And that was great, you know, that was really good. I quickly realized that I've just gotta do things really quickly and spontaneously and try not to get too intensely involved in it. I think that's why I did a lot of the early writing, early recording – I'd get an idea, you know, sat outside having a coffee, and I'd come straight down and just try and do it without learning it, just put it down as quick as I could – cause I knew it's really important to be kind of – just really expressive, and...just sort of quite straight-up, quite honest. So I really enjoyed doing that, and I think you don't do that sometimes, when there're other people around, and someone else gets involved, and they have a view on it, and it's like, "maybe you should try it on this instrument", and they're sort of, "oh no, it'd be much better on that", and you know, all these disagreements about how to begin recording something. So all of that was removed, and I think it really helped to keep me focused.

MW: **That finding your voice thing is really interesting. I wonder if that's a forever ongoing process – like, it may be that you find your voice for this album, but maybe your voice is different for the next.**

GC: Definitely, definitely. Although...when I look back now, I think there were maybe the songs that were just more me. In a way, that was my voice at that time [...] I was interested to see what the concentrated version of myself was.

MW: **It was a long career that Supergrass had, and you were very young when you started, so that must have been interesting, not really having done anything else before that, apart from a couple of other bands...**

GC: Yeah. I don't regret anything or wish I'd done anything differently – I mean maybe it would have been great to sort of do an album of my own or with somebody else at some point through the career, but the demands were always so much each year, you know, you're either in the studio or you're on the road, and the in between time is just very short, so it always seemed hard to do any extra things. But no, it is weird. I think about that... yeah, there was nothing before. There was no time for me just to sort of... I don't know, do loads of really crappy gigs on my own, and then think, "oh, fuck, I need a band", you know? It was sort of like, it all happened straight away.

I mean, I'm really kind of keen that it's not, that it's never taken as a sort of cathartic thing or a sort of, you know, something I had to do – it's just that after finishing the band, I just kind of kept coming down here and writing... it's just sort of what I do, it's like, you don't stop painting because you lose your agent or whatever, you just keep doing what you love doing, and whatever is on the periphery of life or around, that just changes around you, and you always just keep on the same page in a way, you know.

MW: That's one of the things that we're hoping to look at in the book – the idea that you do just want to do this thing, you know, whether it's writing, or music, or art, or whatever. And the logistics of it are often ridiculous, but that doesn't necessarily stop people from doing it.

GC: No, no, definitely. And I'm too old to have grown out of it, or to even have thought about growing out of it at any point, it's not gonna happen. So I will still be doing it as an old fella, or in some different shape – whether it's production, or being a musician, or film scoring, you know. The interesting thing is actually there's a lot I haven't done. I haven't got a film score that I'm really into – there's been offers in the past, but nothing that I really was that into. So that would be amazing to do. So there's always things, you know, that you haven't done, that you can look towards.

MW: I wonder what your thoughts are on independence, and whether that can work longer term; you know, bands who sell their music online, produce their own stuff – do they eventually have to become part of the system, or do you reckon that's a viable way of doing music?

GC: I don't know. I think it could always start there, but I don't know. I mean, there are a few examples, but the first one I can think of is Arctic Monkeys. When the Myspace thing was kind of peaking and they had a huge online following, they were releasing early bits online, and I mean I suppose it's just the nature of the business, and it's the same with other kind of areas of art, that to take it to the next level you kind of inevitably need someone who's gonna be able to play with all the big boys and, you know, get TV stuff and move it up on radio … or it'll get to a certain size online and then it'll be snapped up by someone … because you know, ultimately, if it goes that well online, and you get tens or hundreds of thousands of followers in that way, then you're kind of set for the big time anyway. I dunno, it's weird. It's a tricky one.

MW: **I guess it depends on what your aims are – whether fame is the object, or whether you just want to be able to stay in one place and feed yourself …**

GC: I think for me it kind of ranges. I think in general I'm sort of like, I just want to keep doing what I'm doing, you know, without getting another job, that's great. And I think it's quite simple really, like that. But then I think when you write some really good music, or when you finish a record and think, oh I'm really, really happy with my record, I just really kind of love the way it's turned out, and then I start thinking well fuck, you know, yeah, it could go anywhere, I'm up for it doing really fucking well, you know, and I just sort of think why not, I just think I really want people to be able to hear it. And I know what my limits are, I know what I don't want to do, I've had 20 years of preparing for that sort of stuff. So you know, I think there will always be those points where you pull it back, but at the same time, I'm up for seeing what could happen, seeing how far it could go.

MW: **Yeah, you'd have to be crazy to say, "oh, well, I don't want people to listen to this"! Although I suppose there are people who do very specialist things, really niche things, who don't expect or want to be heard on a big scale, necessarily.**

GC: I think quite often, if it's sort of underground, and not many people know of it, it's often, you know, it's like the coolest thing. But I dunno, it's really hard to see where the underground is these days, because things are being done in an underground sort of fashion, like online stuff, but if they're really good, they'll just get loads of fuckin' hits and become really popular. So I don't know, were they underground for like 10, 20 minutes? Whereas you know, back in the 70s and 80s, there'd be bands sort of floating around doing records that tons of people wouldn't have heard of, and you find them sort of 10, 15 years later and go, "I can't believe I never heard of that band at the time!" It seemed a lot easier to remain under the radar back then.

MW: Yeah, I suppose it's easy — well, it's easier now to kind of shout about yourself.

GC: But then also, there's a real saturation of stuff, you know, with bands and singer/songwriters all over the internet. It means that it gives people the freedom to put out some really awful stuff as well. It's like, it's a double-edged thing — it's amazing, the freedom of creativity and, you know, immediately putting it up for people to hear — it can unearth something incredible stuff, but equally, kind of, a thousand of the same kinds of shit.

MW: I guess it's always been that way, but people were in their parents' basement or something, so you wouldn't necessarily have access to it.

GC: Well you'd have a cassette, and how can you upload that to millions of people, you know, there's just no way of doing it. So the cassette would have to get around school, then someone would take it off to a different city, and then it'd go around ... you know. But I dunno. I really feel split about it, I feel like it's a totally double-edged thing. I really see the positives, but I think the negative side, the sort of over-saturation of stuff, can be just a bit of a headache.

MW: I also think sometimes these kind of more undergroundy bands get a fan base who only like them because they're not known, and because there's a connection — a sense that you're supporting the underdog. And there's a threshold, which probably changes depending on your circumstances, but there's definitely a threshold where you end up losing people because you've become bigger.

GC: Yeah. But I think you could sort of overcome that in a way. I dunno, I like to think maybe we kind of did overcome a bit of that sort of thing with the first few records, just through sort of changing, after the first record, and doing something that probably appeared at first to be sort of self-destructive, cause we didn't do another Alright, you know, we kind of changed it and made it a bit darker. And I dunno, I think that's a good message to your fans, is that you know, we're not sort of coming to the big machine – we're really happy because we're 17 and we're touring the world and everything's going really well, but we're gonna just do this weird dark music because we can, and because everyone is really into us at the moment, so fuck it. I think that's the way you keep those initial fans – because then they feel like they're part of it, that you're doing it for them, rather than the machine, you know, the huge sort of corporate record company. I think there's a lot of bands that have done that, over the years, that have just managed to keep reacting to the last album. But I don't think there's enough of that sort of thing. You know, Coldplay and stuff, Snow Patrol – I've met them all as people, and they're really nice guys, it's hard to sort of slag a band off, but I do find it really kind of, yeah, strange, that there's no changing, there's no sort of evolving, really.

MW: **I think it feels quite unnatural, because people are inclined to be changing, both artistically and personally, and circumstances are changing, and your life is not the same as it was a year ago no matter what's happened. So I think maybe it feels to me like these bands that produce the same kind of record every year, or every couple of years – it just doesn't feel as genuine.**

GC: Yeah, definitely, it's got the sort of formula … and this is the thing, in a way, it's also the fans' fault in terms of not being fussy. Maybe when it gets to that level of Coldplay or whatever, you get people that aren't actually that into music, they're like radio listeners, just kind of if a song comes on they're like, "oh, I like this". So I suppose we were talking before about the underground sort of fans, and that sort of following, and they're probably sort of real music fans, know all about different sorts of music, so they can appreciate what you're doing. But I suppose on that big level, the big commercial sort of U2-sized bands, you know, you get a lot of fans that are just not fussy. So they'll probably be happy with the same U2 each time. Although actually they [U2] do sort of chop and change a little bit. But yeah, yeah. It's a strange one.

MW: When I first saw Little Fish perform, they were very much doing the real rock 'n' roll kind of thing, and it's interesting having seen them change over the last couple of years. And I wonder what their fans think – you know, they probably do have fans who think, "oh, well, this isn't what I signed up for, I like when Jules is screaming down the mic, I don't wanna hear Ben playing a harmonica and them doing some acoustic thing" – but you also get incredibly supportive people who very much want to see what happens.

GC: Yeah, definitely. And that's how I feel about Jules and Ben. With Jules, you know, for me, it's all just about her voice. She's an incredible character, great personality, great on stage, and she's got this amazing voice. I don't give a shit if she's screaming or like, singing as soft as, like, a whispering vocal – it's Jules' voice, and it's amazing either way. I'd be really interested actually to see what she sounds like, cause we've worked together you know a fair bit, to see what she sounds like kind of – I mean, not ultra soft, but kind of more melodic, and kind of using the softness of her voice a bit more, kind of like a modern sort of Velvet Undergroundy sort of vibe, just sort of, I dunno, with different sort of energy – there are moments in songs where she goes fuckin' insane, but add dynamics, I think it's gotta have dynamics … and yeah, right at the beginning I think they were just kind of very raucous, and still amazing, but I think they could have more dimensions.

MW: At one of the Rotunda gigs that you did in December, the one where Little Fish were supporting, they did a song with a ukulele, which I think they'd written the day before or something, and that was really interesting, because it didn't sound like anything I'd ever heard Jules sing before, but I actually really liked it.

GC: Yeah, it was really good. And the first song, when she walked around without the mic, you know, that's great, that's really kind of quite a cool little contemporary move. But anyway, I just think that – I would imagine Little Fish fans, if they're like me, and I'm a fan, would just be like, come on, just hit me with it, throw it at me, I'm waiting to hear what you do next, I know that as long as you're singing, it's gonna be great.

MW: I think that seems to be the general kind of feeling. Like you said, it's about the voice more than anything else, and so whatever that voice is doing is going to be of interest.

GC: Well that's it, and I'm just sort of really, you know, I get really frustrated when I think back […] I dunno, I suppose they got a glimpse, and maybe they felt they got a shot, a shot at maybe making it big, and I think she just, Linda Perry just got it wrong, and it's a real shame that it's kinda fucked them up a bit…

But I think they should totally be given the space and the chance to sort of to prove it again, and I think it's just a shame that… you know, I suppose like journalists will sort of already have a bit of knowledge about Little Fish, which is sort of possibly negative – you know, they'll be starting from there, and they shouldn't be, they should start from now. It's like, they've only done one album. Bands can get to sort of three, four, five albums and still not quite get there. So anyway.

MW: It's interesting as you get older, you know, and you're not 18 and playing in a basement anymore, and maybe it's hard to think about your musical career in the same myopic way that you do when you don't feel like everything's riding on it.

GC: Yeah, definitely, definitely. It is hard when you get a bit older, and you're sort of quite lucky to have stuff in place… I dunno, I mean, I've got two kids and so there are a lot more thoughts about kind of just keeping things going. It does change slightly the way you think about things when you're older, but I dunno, what I'm not great at is I still keep just refusing things. I mean, I could make more of it, but I think I'm just happy the way that it is, and if it means that, you know, you might be feeling a bit sort of pressured about money or whatever, you have to just deal with it. I'd rather sleep well.

MW: So you said the new record comes out in May?

GC: Yeah, now it's just preparation for live stuff. It's kind of weird not having a band. But it's kind of exciting, you know, it's been really interesting doing that and also being inspired by what's around. […] I've really enjoyed trying to look forward a bit, not resting on techniques that I've learned over the years and ways of doing things – it'd be nice to sort of move forward, see if I can expand my voice a bit.

MW: Right. And you get to do it all here?

GC: Yeah, pretty much. I worked with Sam actually as well, Sam Williams, who's a producer. We produced it together, and he was brilliant for helping it to sound better. He's great at mixing, but also at just sort of keeping me up as well ... there were definitely a few times I remember last year where I was feeling the strain of it all a little bit, and you have a few bad days and you get really negative about all of it and you feel really lethargic about the whole process. And he'd sort of be there going "look, you're on the brink of a fucking great record, man", you know, and it's so good to have someone like that to remind you.

MW: **Especially when you're doing something on your own, it's good to have somebody spurring you on.**

GC: Totally, yeah, exactly. So that was great, when I brought him in to be part of it like that and it really, really worked. And yeah, great to just be able to sit down here and work on some crazy ideas, and it's there, it's all done you know, it's kind of ... yeah ... like a bedroom musician. Yeah, I need to actually get Little Fish in here soon, you know, Jules and Ben, just to do some stuff, it'd be great, see if we can do some crazy new songs ...

MW: **It's nice that Oxford is small and supportive enough that you get these kind of overlaps and collaborations.**

GC: Yeah, definitely. It struck me at the Rotunda actually – I think Spring Offensive [who supported Gaz at a gig there the night before Little Fish supported him] as well, I really like them, I think they're great, I mean I'm doing a bit of mixing for them next week down here, and yeah – two bands I really really rate, there's definitely some really cool stuff going on in Oxford. And yeah, I'd love it if my record was completely Oxford-made, even down to the mastering ... 100% made in Oxford.

MW: **Yeah, I like that. You think of the stereotypical successful band, you know, they move off to the big city, they get all these anonymous people to work on their stuff – but it's nice if there's a more personal element.**

GC: Yeah, totally. You know, I never really saw a reason to move away from Oxford; obviously we were doing a lot of touring back then as well, so I suppose we did move away in a sense, because we just sort of moved onto a tour bus for like nine years, ten years. But great having Oxford always here when we got back.

But yeah, it's great those sort of early days. I remember it really fondly, when you just start to get your following up, and then you know that you get to a point where you can headline the Jericho, and then you know that from then on it's always going to be like that – but then it's either gonna stay like that or get better, and it's an amazing feeling. I remember our first headline show, and everyone's just kind of going mental and moshing, and it was a really mad feeling. It was kind of like, "shit, I think we might have done it, I think we've really got somewhere". And I think that's still relevant now, you know. Apart from the Oxford venues aren't quite as characterful as they once were. Or maybe it's just rose tinted glasses.

ROBERT ROSENBERG

Robert Rosenberg has managed Little Fish for the last few years under the umbrella of Trinifold Management, who have also managed The Who, Robert Plant, and Judas Priest. Robert and I spoke in May of 2012 at his office in London. (NB. he refers to Juju as "Jules" in the interview, and Nez as "Neil".)

Miranda Ward: Can you give me a little bit of background about how you got into this – a sort of potted career history?

Robert Rosenberg: I'm a qualified accountant, and I got a job when I was very young working at a place called the William Morris office, which is a theatrical agency. And I was their accountant, but I was also very interested in music, because I played in a band at school, and I was obsessed with my music, as most people were in those days. And after I'd been there for five years I got offered a job by a record producer who I'd met through working there, who was producing an artist called David Essex – he was really big in the mid- to late 70s in England – he was huge, a bit like a sort of Justin Bieber of his day. So I went into business with him for a couple of years, and then I got offered a songwriting deal, by a guy I'd been in a band with at school. He ran a studio, and I went into his studio to do demos – I thought, well, I'm only gonna be able to do this once in my life, so I sort of packed up my job and just asked around – do you know anyone who needs a part-time accountant? Just to get a bit of money coming in. And they said, "oh, this guy, Bill

Curbishley, manager of The Who, at Trinifold" – so I started off going in three mornings a week, just doing the books, and then over the years got more and more involved.

MW: **What do you feel has changed about the music industry since you started out?**

RR: I can take you back to the late 70s. Before that, I feel the industry was much more of an artistic industry. There were artists, and there were people running record companies who were – obviously they wanted to make money, but they were much more music people, you know. A lot of the people that ran record companies were ex-musicians, songwriters, whatever. And also the A&R people. It was a very artistic industry. It nurtured artists, and the artists that it nurtured, a lot of them are still around today.

And then in the mid- to late 70s, with the punk explosion, there came people into the industry, such as the journalists who started writing about music – and suddenly you had to be relevant, you had to be this, you had to be that. And a lot of people who I knew at the time got very frightened by that, because they were basically just musos, you know, who were writing songs and making music, and suddenly all these bands of the 70s were like dinosaurs. And I think the whole record industry's never really been the same since, you know, since music became about the subject matter and the attitude and the fashion and style rather than the actual music.

You know, I was talking about this to someone – we were trying to think of, since sort of 1980, how many British artists are there that are worldwide stars, household names? And we could only come up with half a dozen – you know, Coldplay, Radiohead, George Michael, I can't remember who the others were, but – Adele, obviously, is the latest one, Amy Winehouse – but you know, when you consider it's 30 years ... So that's the main change, that it became much more about the bottom line, you know. You've still got some ex-artists and songwriters running labels, and other people with really good ears, but they seem much too constrained by the reality of the business to be able to just let artists develop over a number of albums. The record labels all became multinational corporations, got absorbed, all the labels got absorbed into the bigger corporations, and now it's getting smaller and smaller. You've got Universal buying EMI, and you've got Sony and you've got Warner, and the rest of it is mainly independent labels. So that is the main change.

If you go into the financial side of it, once the internet started, and downloading and all the various other things that supposedly took money away – well, there are two views. One is that the internet and downloading ruined the industry because nobody bought CDs anymore – nobody spent money on records because everybody was getting everything for free. The other argument is that if there's something that people actually like, they'll still buy it. So is it [a decline in album sales] due to the fact that the product just isn't good enough? You know, if I was working for Marks & Spencer, and suddenly my sales dropped by 25%, I would immediately think, "well, people don't like my product, I've gotta do something about that".

Obviously there are a lot more distractions for kids now. Music used to be everything to people and now it's not; there are lots of other things out there. But I've got two daughters who are teenagers, and they're obsessed by music, almost as much as I was. So it's still out there, there's just lots of other stuff that also takes up the space. And also the kind of people I think that are going into music now – you have the people of the 60s who went into music because that's what everybody did, everybody formed a band, you know, went to art college and then formed a band, and they expected it to last a couple years. Now if people are becoming musicians, they're looking at it and going, "well, the odds against me actually making any money are thousands to one. Is it a good career for me? No, I'll become a computer programmer, or a this or a that". So probably a lot of those sort of genius types who could have become the next Pete Townshend or Bob Dylan, they now do something else.

MW: **And anyway the money in music isn't necessarily in records, is it, unless you sell tons of them?**

RR: No. It used to be – that's the thing. First of all, the retail price of a record used to be much higher, and you'd get paid a royalty on that retail price, and you sold far more. Now the price has gone way down, and you sell far less, so obviously there's less money. And the cost used to be astronomically high – you used to get people doing a video for a quarter of a million pounds and things like that, which probably happens to half a dozen artists now in the world, you know. But it was fairly routine, in the 80s and 90s, to spend huge amounts of money just doing a video – you'd go out to a desert in Morocco or somewhere and take a load of people. Because there was so much money floating around. And now it's just not there.

MW: So how can a band or a musician make a career out of it – or is it just a luck thing?

RR: If you ask people in the industry, "how do you become successful?" now – you're unlikely to make a lot of money by selling records, unless you're Adele or one of the big acts that really sells a lot of records. Unless you can do it yourself, through your own label or your own imprint, where your margin is much higher. But if you're doing it going through a major label, the costs that'll be charged back to you, the recording costs and everything else, unless you can do it really economically, you're very unlikely to make a meaningful amount of money. Which is why to be a manager these days is a really tough job, because you're then getting a percentage of that, and if it's not a meaningful amount of money… So most managers are probably operating from home or from their car and mobile phone. And it is very tough to make money. Music publishing is still quite lucrative. You get money when your music's played on the radio or in public or whatever. That's still quite lucrative, and touring is lucrative once you get past a certain level, because the touring industry's still reasonably healthy, although that seems to be changing a little bit. And if you can get your music onto an ad, or you can get it into a movie, that's still very lucrative.

But the other interesting area of the business is merchandising. If you become an iconic brand – those brands are making a huge amount of money. Some of them are making more money on t-shirts and clothing than they're making out of records. You also get pop acts like One Direction and people like that making millions out of merchandising and the expectation is that'll be a short-term thing, maybe a few years if they're lucky, but they can make a huge amount of money on merchandising in those few years that they're popular.

But a band, a young band, even a band that becomes reasonably successful, they don't sell a lot of t-shirts. And that's an interesting thing, because it somehow represents what is gone from the industry, which is the mystique, the idea that people wanna walk around with something on their chest that is iconic. If you go down to Camden Market, you know, you'll see Bob Dylan, Amy Winehouse, Jim Morrison, Abbey Road, all these iconic images. But you won't see a band that's in the charts. The people that do the merchandise are sort of struggling to work out how to make a brand out of a young, new act. And it's very difficult, because you know too much about them. They're not mysterious enough. That's my feeling anyway.

MW: So how do you feel about the less traditional options available to independent artists – crowdfunding an album via Kickstarter, or selling music on Bandcamp, things like that?

RR: I think any idea like that is fantastic. You know, I think there are more talented musicians around today than there have been for years. People come in and play me stuff, and I hear stuff, and there're just some incredible people out there. And you look at it and you go, well, what could I actually do? And obviously we've taken on Little Fish, we've taken on Paul Freeman, and we're looking at another artist to take on at the moment, a singer-songwriter. And they're all incredibly talented people, and you look at all sorts of ways to try and break them. Kids who are coming up with these kinds of ideas, it's great, but when you talk to people in the major record labels, who are supposedly the people who know where it's at, they say it's still all about getting on the radio, or getting onto something like Jools Holland, or something like that, which sort of shortcuts everything. I know I've said this to Jules, and she hates me for it. I was talking to a manager recently who had a band that had six million hits on its YouTube video, but he said that if their record didn't get on the Radio 1 playlist the following Monday they were gonna get dropped. So the internet somehow doesn't translate into sales in a lot of cases.

MW: Do you think there's a future for musicians who want to do it completely on their own, whose goal isn't to then be signed by a major label?

RR: Well, I think you can't get signed by a major label unless you're already sort of a going concern. You know, if you go to a major label, which is what we're trying to do here, to get Little Fish and Paul and this other girl we might be signing to a point where a record label might be interested in them – in order to do that you've gotta have radio play. I mean the record companies still look at how many people have looked at your YouTube, although they're now realizing that doesn't actually mean much. But they're still looking at that. You know, in the old days you'd ring up a record label and go, "I've got this great artist, can I come and play you the CD?" Whereas now they go "oh, have they got a Myspace, have they got a YouTube". In the old days – I keep saying the old days, it's not that long ago! – they would go to Hull or Leicester or Leeds or wherever, go and see a band play. Now you can't even get them out into Camden, you know, because everything's available to them on the internet. So if you've got a gig and you want to get people out to it, it's a struggle. Because the record companies are really only looking for artists that already have something going on. So it's essential as a new artist to develop yourself to that point before you approach a record label, in my opinion.

MW: **Do you think that a band has to have a hit to be successful?**

RR: I don't know what you mean by a hit these days! But I think – it's pretty much essential, yeah. Unless you're gonna build up some incredible live following, like a Dave Matthews Band. I mean that's the ideal scenario. The difference between somebody that buys a record and somebody that goes to a gig – you know, the person that goes to a gig is actually a proper fan. The person that buys the record isn't – they just bought it because they like the record. So if you're putting bums on seats, that is the surest sign that you've got a long-term future. And you get a lot of artists who have a huge record, and they'll put tickets on sale and nobody comes. And that's it. I won't give you any names, but I can think of loads of them over the last few years. As my partner Bill says, you never know what's out there, when you put tickets on sale. It's very scary. Because you think you're gonna sell a lot of tickets and you don't, or you get pleasantly surprised.

MW: **Do you think that musicians should approach their career from the viewpoint of a businessman or an artist?**

RR: I think they should always approach it from the point of view of an artist. You know, I got an email – my daughter's at school, and there's a boy she knows who's 16, and he sent me an email with all these questions. And the first question is, "we do all sorts of music, what's the gap in the market at the moment?" And I said to him, if that's the way you're thinking, you're finished. You should do what you do, what you feel passionate about, and that's all you should ever do. And if you try and exploit the marketplace people will see through you pretty quickly. And if you try and exploit the marketplace chances are by the time you've got something out, the marketplace will have moved on to something else.

So I think being an artist is way more important, because it's a sort of emotional thing, music. Being a businessman helps, but sometimes it can also get in the way. I've seen people ruin their careers, artists who are too involved in business and too interested in it, and have turned things down for financial reasons which really they should have taken. I always say that 50 percent of something's better than a 100 percent of nothing. I've seen people be offered deals which weren't that great, and I've said to them look, it's not a great deal, but if you don't take it you'll never get another deal. And they've passed it up, and never been heard of since.

So sometimes it's a bad thing to be too much of a businessman, but you need good advisors. And again that's difficult because they cost money, and you can't always afford to have good advisors. But there are a lot of people like me in business who'll give kids advice, just for the sake of it. I get loads of people asking for advice, as do a lot of managers, I'm sure. And there're also, to be fair, a lot of lawyers who will work and put it on the slate. So it's not as difficult as it seems to get good advisors. I would always say to people, get a good advisor, and you concentrate on the music.

MW: **How did you come to manage Little Fish?**

RR: What happened was, a friend of mine rang me one day and said "I've just started this business management company and we've got all these artists who've got no management", and he sent me like five links, and one of them was Little Fish. It was the only one I liked. So I went back and said "they sound great", and he said, "oh, I shouldn't have sent you that, they've got management, blah blah blah". But I noticed that they were doing a gig in Camden a couple of nights later, so I went down anyway to see them. And I thought they were great, thought, oh, it's a shame I can't get involved, and then forgot about them. And about a year later, maybe even longer, an agent in California who's a friend of mine rang me up and said, "there's this band we've got looking for management, are you interested?" And I couldn't believe it was the same band, it was really amazing – of all the thousands of bands! So I said oh, I know them, they're great. So that was really how it happened. And I went and met them in Oxford, met Jules and Neil.

MW: **What was it that you liked about them?**

RR: When they came to me they had a finished album, which I loved. I loved the fact that it had really passionate great lyrics, great sound, Linda Perry, obviously, great person, great producer – and I just loved the music, and I'd seen them play live already, and that was really it. The way we are as a company is that we basically take stuff on that we like. We don't go, is this fashionable, is it not, is it this, is it that, which probably most managers would do. I think we go into every project with a new artist not expecting to make any money. You know, in this day and age, you're not quite getting into it for philanthropic reasons, but you're going into it hoping that you can create something that will eventually become successful, and eventually you might make some money out of it, but really we took them on because we just really love the music, that was it.

MW: **So how do you feel about the way their music has changed or developed over the years?**

RR: Well, I think the experience with the label was – it wasn't disastrous, it was just unfortunate that it was a period of time where the business was contracting, and the funding available to the label was not as good as it was. The first album never got released in America, which is a terrible shame, it never really got any worthwhile promotion over there. Here we managed to get Island Records to do a little bit on it, and they developed it a little bit here, they did some fantastic touring work, which we got in 2009 or 2010, a lot of which was down to Linda Perry and the label – they did one tour after another, and they were seen by a lot of people here, and they were really at the point when they could have had a really successful second album. And then they parted company with the record company – which was obviously very traumatic for Jules and Neil. But for me it's the kind of thing I've seen many, many times before, unfortunately. And then with Ben coming into the mix, the music changed inevitably, and now with Neil going out of the mix it's changed even more, and that's the reality of it. And so if you're saying, if they'd come into my office now with what they're doing now would I be interested? I'm not a 100 percent sure, because I've only heard a couple of the new songs. I liked what they did in Paris with the new line-up. And I think Jules is a major talent. And we'll just have to see how it all develops.

MW: **What do you think their future might look like?**

RR: It goes back to what I said before – she [Jules] should only ever do what she wants to do. There's a difference between a true artist, which I think Jules is, and somebody who's just sort of going with the trend. If you believe in what you do, you've got much more likelihood, although it may take years, of coming through, cutting through. How that will happen, I couldn't tell you. But I've seen incredibly talented people who are in their fifties now, and nothing's ever happened for them. I've seen other people who've had the most ridiculous slice of luck and gone on to be hugely successful. And there's no rhyme or reason to it. We had a guy a couple of years ago who we were involved with for a few months who I thought was very talented, and he had a manager who came and worked for us for a bit, and it seemed to be going nowhere, and we were paying this guy money, and we just thought, *it's not gonna happen*. Three years later, he's now in the top ten. But it's through getting one of his songs on an advert. And now my daughter, you know, she rang me up and asked if I've heard this record, and I said, well, we actually managed him three years ago – I played you his songs and you hated them! So you never know what's gonna happen with anybody. Something can come along and it all changes.

MW: **Do you think that the goal for Little Fish should be to get signed again?**

RR: I don't know about goal. I think it would help. But I don't think it's essential. Another artist who we've got has got onto a major BBC radio playlist, which is what we've been trying to achieve with Little Fish, and hopefully will achieve, get them onto some major playlist. As soon as that happened, people started phoning up, going oh, yeah, what's going on, has he got a publishing deal, you know – whereas before, I'd been mentioning it to people and playing it and they weren't interested. So we've got to try and make something happen, or the band have got to try and make something happen. Somebody has got to get that profile going for them, so that if they want to be signed by a major label, the label's gonna look and go "wow, something's going on here". The days of taking a CD of an unknown artist and getting a multi-hundred-thousand-dollar kind of record deal because they like it – that doesn't happen anymore. Well, it probably does somewhere, but they need to know there's something going on before they take that risk, because they can't afford to otherwise.

MW: **What's the advantage that a band who's signed to a major label – or any label, really – will have?**

RR: It's really to do with marketing. The record labels now – the main advantage for an artist is that they have the ability to market you in a much bigger way. I suppose TV and radio and people like that still take more notice of an artist on a major label than they do of somebody on some small label. If someone at Sony or Universal goes in to TV or radio and goes we've got this person, they're a major priority for us, blah blah blah, they're gonna listen to that more closely than they will if some plugger goes in there with an artist that isn't signed. It's just the reality of life. So it helps. And once you've got something going on – in other words, if you get a record in the charts or something – then the major label can roll it out in a much bigger way through their marketing clout and put you in places where you might not be able to go if you were doing it on your own. But having said that, you know, Adele was on an independent label. I still believe it's all about quality of music, and if you've got great music and you can get it to people to hear it, you'll sell records. And that will never change. The public know great music when they hear it.

MW: **How influential is the music press?**

RR: They are influential. They don't actually sell anything anymore, but what I've seen happen, especially with Little Fish, is that the people at radio take note of what the NME and people like that like. If you're on the front cover of NME, then suddenly Radio 1 or 2 will look at it and go, oh, that's interesting. So they do have an influence on what gets played. I think NME only sells like 25,000, 30,000 copies now, so I dunno that they have that much of an influence on what people actually buy themselves, but they have an influence on the gatekeepers of the industry, as I call them, the radio producers and TV producers and A&R people at record companies, who are sort of the people that control what music people are allowed to hear. They read those magazines.

MW: **Can you imagine that things might change to such an extent that the gatekeepers have significantly less power? Do you think that people are going to spend more time looking for their own music online?**

RR: The trouble with online is that there's so much music. Where do you start? The gatekeepers, as I call them, the people at radio, hear what's put in their faces. They have probably hundreds of tracks a week to listen to from pluggers. And they go with what they like. But if you go online there're just so many thousands and thousands of bands and artists. You'll get the occasional phenomenon, a Justin Bieber or somebody who has millions of people looking at him. But it's something that everybody's trying to work out, to be honest with you – how to best use the internet. With Little Fish, you know, we got their album five-star reviews on loads of these websites, and it makes not a jot of difference. It seems to be still all about people hearing the music and liking it and going out and buying it. And that is a call you have to make, if you think what you've got is going to appeal to the public. So we'll see.

BEN WALKER

Ben has played Hammond for Little Fish since 2010, but he's been a musician in some form for most of his life. I interviewed him at home in late summer 2012.

Miranda Ward: How and why did you become a musician?

Ben Walker: Becoming a musician is a strange one. I always did music, I always played musical instruments and I always liked music – it was the one thing I was really good at. So it kind of just happened, really. I think that was about as complicated as it got. I suppose the other key part is that I never really did anything else too enthusiastically. I had other jobs and did other things, but music was always there. So I suppose that's it, really – I just did it for long enough that I was, eventually, a musician.

MW: Were you making money from your music before you joined Little Fish?

BW: I played music for money for the first time, I think, when I was 14 – playing dinner jazz with some friends from school. And for the next ten years I did various gigs like that – I did lots of dinner jazz, I did wedding bands, I did teaching, I did anything I could think of, really. I did all those things for some money – never all of my living, but bits and bobs. And then I did quite a bit of other music as well, writing my own songs, being in various bands, playing with various bands, playing sessions with various bands. I think I just always grasped every opportunity to do some music without any real plan, basically.

MW: **How were you introduced to Little Fish?**

BW: I was introduced to Little Fish twice. The first time was when I went to The Borderline in London to see my friend Jont play a solo gig, and Little Fish was I think supporting – might have been the other way round, but I think Little Fish was supporting Jont at that gig, and it was just Jules on her own. And she'd sprained her wrist, so she turned up with a guitar but she couldn't play the guitar – she started playing the first song and just said, "sorry, I can't do it, I'm gonna have to stop". And everyone was so enchanted by the first 30 seconds of her song that they were cheering, "no, no no, carry on, carry on!" So eventually she carried on and did the whole gig just acapella, for about 20 minutes or so, a whole set. And you could have heard a pin drop in the place. It was magical. So that was the first time – and I didn't meet Jules then, she ran away straight after the gig, claimed it was terrible.

And then, a few years later, I was playing piano with Jont, the same guy, in his band, and we had a rehearsal in Oxford, and he'd invited Jules to come and sing on one of his recordings, to just come and try singing some stuff over one of the songs to see if it would work. So she turned up at the rehearsal at about midnight one night, I think she'd had a Little Fish rehearsal beforehand. She turned up in the middle of our practice, and as soon as she walked in, she looked at me and said, "do you play Hammond?" And I said yes. She said "great, what's your phone number?" And I gave her my phone number, and she said, "alright, sorry, hello everyone!" It turned out she'd been looking for a Hammond player for a year or so, and tried various people, so she was very excited to see someone playing any kind of keyboard. And that was that really. She came and recorded the track with Jont, which I don't think ever got used for anything but sounded cool at the time. And I joined the band a couple of weeks later.

MW: **What's your idea of success – both for yourself and for Little Fish?**

BW: I was thinking about this earlier, and I still don't know whether I'll ever be able to really figure it out. But I think – personally, my idea of success is being able to do interesting things with my time. To come up with interesting ideas and plans and talk to people about them and then sometimes do them. Because I play a lot of music and like music and am quite good at it, the plans tend to involve music somehow. But sometimes it's making magazines or doing other things. So I think that's it: just doing interesting things with my time is my idea of success.

I think as far as Little Fish goes, it's more complicated, because there are more people to think about. I know that Jules's idea of success, and our manager's idea of success, and everyone we work with – they all have a slightly different idea of success. Lots of them are not the same as mine, because most of the other people involved are trying to make money from whatever project we're doing. That's not really my priority. So I guess with Little Fish, it's similar, but I think my real idea of success for Little Fish would be to – how do I say this? – to kind of – to do justice to the whole Little Fish thing that Jules has created. I think that's it. She came up with Little Fish as a solo thing, and then it was with Nez, and then with me and Nez, and then with me, and now with the others – but it's always been the same thing: Jules has an idea, a creative idea, and she's always trying to express it in new and different ways. I think every time – well, maybe we get a little bit closer to that, but I don't think it's something that you – I don't think it's something we'll achieve and go "oh, great, now that's done!" I think it's a lifelong mission, to just be Little Fish. And obviously that has lots of implications. We need some money to live and we need people to work with and we need people to be able to get something out of it themselves so that they'll want to work with us and do different things – so you know, it's not quite as pure as my own way of doing things.

MW: **What's the most enjoyable bit of music, for you?**

BW: For me I think it's all enjoyable in different ways. I think the song-writing tends to be the hardest bit – it's the bit that's most frustrating, but therefore most satisfying when it works (which it always does, eventually). Rehearsing is really satisfying in a social way. It's really nice hanging out with a band and working stuff out and getting things right and getting better – that's all fun. And performing is certainly the most thrilling of the three – the adrenaline of performing, whether it's with Little Fish or doing my own little songs, or anything really, even just playing in the lounge with some friends. Performing is always quite thrilling.

MW: **What's the most difficult part?**

BW: I think writing is the hardest part. Performing's hard, but I've had 25 years of practice and now I'm quite good at it, so I don't have to think about that too much anymore. But writing is always as hard, every time you do it, whether it's writing myself or helping Jules out with stuff, or working on stuff that she's written – but it's always a satisfying struggle.

MW: **Do you think it's harder or easier nowadays to make a life or a career out of music than it was, say, 20 years ago?**

BW: I don't know. My idea of music 20 years ago – I was 12. So as far as I was concerned, it was really easy – you just had to be like Vanilla Ice or something. Life seemed pretty easy for him at the time. Like, it proved not to be in the end, I guess – didn't he get arrested? But I don't know – it's really difficult to know how much of the mythology around the music industry before we had the internet and before we had all the stuff that we have now – how much of that was true. I think for people who were musicians 20 years ago and making money then, it's probably harder for them now, because the things that were working for them at the time probably don't work for them so much now. So I think that's true. Apart from that, I think it's probably just as hard in different ways.

MW: **I wanted to ask you to speak a little bit about the "industry" – are there aspects of it that are good for musicians? What bits are not so good for musicians?**

BW: It has its positives and negatives, I guess. Personally, I don't think much of the machine is much good for musicians. I don't think much of it is. But I think to exist as a band completely outside of it does cut you off from not just the useful bits like the press and distribution and radio and stuff, which is all part of a huge interlinked web of businesses – but also from the majority of music listeners, who don't realize that music exists outside of that world. You know, it does put you out on a bit of an island, and you have to be willing to be happy with that position and work hard to keep things going.

MW: Do you think that's possible for bands, though? I can see how it might work for somebody who does something quite niche, or quite individual – but for a band, a rock band, do you think it's possible to survive on that island?

BW: I think it's possible, but because it's such an awkward question, I think it's a question that's probably going to go away eventually. I think the idea of trying to transfer a rock band, which is quite an old idea, into the digital age probably isn't a great one. It's gonna take another generation to grow up without any rock bands to be happy with that situation – like, I'll never be happy with that situation, because I grew up with bands, and I'm in a band, and obviously I want bands to be able to do what they do. But I think the next generation is not necessarily going to want to carry rock bands through as a special case. Even now, Little Fish has changed the way we do things – we're not really a rock band anymore, and that's not just a style thing. The music's changed a bit, but also it's kind of just me and Jules now. And we're a sort of self-sustaining entity, I guess. We couldn't perform without the other members of the band who play with us, but I think existing as a four-piece band, or a five-piece or a twelve-piece, would be really difficult, and it's just – I suppose it's just not a clever way of doing things. I think you have to be a bit more lean and clever about the way you do things.

MW: What tools and opportunities are there now for independent musicians to take advantage of now? I guess I'm thinking of online stuff, really.

BW: Well, I think the internet is just a way of communicating with lots of people. It's nice that people can do Kickstarter, and it's nice that people can sell stuff on Bandcamp, and it's nice that people can blog freely and put their gigs up, and all that – all of the individual services are really useful. And I'm sure we'll get more and more exciting things as people move away from the idea that everything has to be CDs in shops and everything has to be albums – you know, as those ideas gradually shift, we'll end up with super efficient ways of doing things. None of those things help a band make money on their own, though. You still have to do loads of work and persuade lots of people to buy your music. But you get the chance to actually put your music in front of more people and talk to more people about it, which is all good.

MW: You've recently begun a full-time job after a few years of free-lancing and musician-ing. What's the balance like – between being a musician and having a day job? Do you find that they're compatible?

BW: Yeah, I definitely think they're compatible. But I think it's got to be the right job, and you've got to work very hard. I actually find it a little bit easier to do the music stuff with a full-time job than I did when I was chasing freelance gigs all the time. But I have a lot less time to do the music stuff, you know. Whereas before I could easily sit in the garage for 12 hours a day and fiddle with stuff, now I have a couple of hours a day, or weekends or whatever, to do very specific things. So there's a lot less – play – on the music side at the moment. But that's kind of intentional, I suppose. We made sure that we had most of the next album written, we had the band together, we had all the kind of play parts of it, the creative parts of it, out of the way. So now it's just a case of using the time I have to record demos and to rehearse with the band and to put stuff together. Which is fine, that's doable.

MW: Interesting what you say about it having to be the right job. Because you're doing something that's quite related to the music side of your life, aren't you?

BW: Yeah, absolutely. I'm working for Bandcamp. And I mean – Little Fish has been using Bandcamp since, since I joined, so for a few years. And I've been using Bandcamp pretty much since they started, to sell my little songs. And it's great, it's pretty much my favourite company in the world, and now I'm working for them. So that's really good. Partly because it's great to have a job that you like, but partly because I don't think I could pull off the full-time job and musician combination if I was doing something that left me depleted of energy. The Bandcamp job I find as exciting as doing music.

MW: And also you're able to see it from both sides, aren't you? Because you've used it as an artist yourself.

BW: Yeah, exactly. I spend my days talking to bands who are trying to do cool stuff on the internet, which is great – or to people trying to buy cool music on the internet, which is also great.

MW: Are there any principles that you or Little Fish try to adhere to? Are there things you wouldn't do, even if it meant turning down big opportunities?

BW: Well yeah, there definitely are. I think as I get older there are more and more principles that I adhere to – I don't know whether I'm just becoming more stubborn. I guess they're the same principles that I have in the rest of my life, you know. I like to shop local and to support Bandcamp over major label artists, and I like to – I suppose I just like to think that I'm making hopefully ethical decisions about all the things that I do. And I guess with Little Fish – I don't know if we've really come up against this yet, but if for example we were asked to have our music used in an advert for McDonald's for loads of money, I'd be against that. I think that's going to be different for every band though. If having music in adverts is the way you're going to survive, as a musician, then you might not be able to make those kinds of decisions quite so freely. But hopefully we will.

MW: What do you hope that people get out of Little Fish's music?

BW: I just hope that people get some sort of positive experience out of it. I think when we play live, people tend to really enjoy it, and everyone enjoys it in different ways. I've talked to loads of people about what they like about Little Fish, and they're all different. Some of them like it because it's ROCK! They're gonna be a little disappointed now, I think. But most of them like it just because they recognize something of themselves in what Jules is singing about, or her character, or just her voice or the way the music sounds, the emotion of it. And they like being part of that. I think a lot of it's about the live stuff for me. It's great when people appreciate the stuff that we record, and it's great to hear people talk about it on the internet and go "yay, this is my favourite song!", but what I really like about people's reaction is when it's live and when you see it.

MW: So as a listener yourself, do you get more out of live performances than recorded stuff?

BW: Tricky question. I think the older I get, the more I like live performances. In fact, ideally I like recorded live performances. Gigs don't always sound that great – they're really good fun and the experience is really cool, but my ideal version of most songs is a well-recorded live version. These days, anyway.

MW: **"The older I get"… You're making it sound like you're about a 100 years old!**

BW: Well, I think when you're a teenager you're obsessed with having like a million guitar pedals and everything sounding shiny and amazing. And you're obsessed with gear and audio quality and all of these things that are actually nothing to do with music. They're all to do with *sound*, but they're actually nothing to do with music. I think I've kind of – I don't know whether I've gone past it, I don't know if it's a better thing that I have now, but I've just stopped caring so much about that. I just like stuff that really connects somehow, even if it sounds like crap. In fact, I pretty much prefer it when it sounds like crap. Which is why we're recording the album in a garage.

There's actually a lot of interesting stuff that's going to come out of this next phase of Little Fish, as far as the decisions we make, as far as how much we engage with the industry and the machine and how much we don't. That's going to be an interesting thing. We haven't got any answers to that yet. But the questions are definitely there. We're already a little bit torn between how to finish the album, about how to make it sound – whether to make it sound exactly like it is, like it's recorded in a garage, or whether to mix it better, to make it sound maybe a bit more – accomplished.

MW: **Would the reason to do that simply be because it makes the album more commercially viable?**

BW: No – but I think that'd be a side product of it. I think that's what a lot of managers and agents and people like that would be interested in. But it's more that actually – you record something in the garage and it sounds quite different to what most people are used to hearing on the radio, so there's a chance that you're accidentally alienating a load of people who like music but are just gonna go, "this is some kind of strange weird demo thing". I don't so much care about that, but I spend my days on Bandcamp listening to crazy little cassette bands doing all sorts of stuff that's so lo-fi it's unbearable. So my threshold has moved – I'm probably not the best person to judge it anymore. But yeah, I think that's gonna be interesting. We may end up releasing two versions of the album – the garage version and the industry version!

MW: **Is there anything else you want to add?**

BW: Can everybody please stop putting 30-second snippets of their music online? It's a really bad idea and has been for years.

MW: **Why?**

BW: Because if you stop people listening to your music, they're never going to hear it, basically. Thirty-second snippets only work when you're intentionally stopping people from listening to your music so that they can get really excited about the marketing campaign around it, and then eventually it's released and everyone buys it in one day and then it's in the charts. There is no other reason on earth to do it.

MW: **Isn't this part of a bigger conversation? The whole point of putting a snippet up online is presumably to entice people to buy your music, but there's that "if you give it to people for free they'll just steal it", attitude, right?**

BW: Yeah – it's partly people being worried about people stealing their album. But I think – basically, it makes no sense. I've seen stats on this. Albums with 30-second snippets basically sell nothing. Because every-one goes, "oh, I can only listen to 30 seconds? Well, that's not my favourite album then. I'll try something else." There's lots of music out there. I think once bands get past the whole 90s marketing campaign idea of being mysterious and only having 30-second snippets available and all the rest of it, then the world will be a better place.

The other day I was reading this interview with David Bowie.[35] He did this *Guardian* interview in 1999 – 13 and a half years ago! And he was basi-cally explaining what the internet was – like, "the internet is this great thing for artists! I think it'll be really good for not just digital artists but also people who make ceramics and all sorts of other stuff!" – it was this completely wide-eyed wonder at the internet and what it was going to do. And he'd set up Bowieart.com, which was like his first website, be-fore he even had his own. And this was all cool, he was way ahead of his time. And then he was asked about piracy, and people stealing digital albums. And he was saying, "yeah, you know, the thing is, I think record companies are probably gonna hang on to their way of doing things for a while, because that's what they always do, but you know, we don't have to stay with record companies forever – they're just one way of doing things, and they'll come around". *Thirteen years ago!* He's asked about piracy, and he says, "well, as far as I'm concerned, piracy – it's the way society has evolved, it's kind of destroyed most of our ideas of intellectual copyright, and whether that's a good or bad thing is largely moot, because that's just the way it's happened. So I tend to basically ignore piracy and get on with trying to make music for people." *Thirteen years ago!* And still people say something like that now and get shouted down. It's amazing.

JUJU

The following interview with Juju was compiled over the course of several recorded conversations in the late spring of 2012.

Miranda Ward: When you first began writing and performing, did you think it was something you might want to do as a living, or did that desire develop over time?

JUJU: I never had any sense of that. I started writing songs because I was attracted to the music block at school. I used to creep in to the lessons. And the teacher would allow me, but after a while he kept me after class and told me, "if you want to be part of the lessons, you're going to have to start joining in with the homework". I couldn't play an instrument, and you had to be able to play an instrument. That week, the homework was to write a song using seventh chords. I remember one of my friends going, "it's really easy to learn the guitar, look at me, I just got this book and learned some chords". And so I went home that day, borrowed a guitar, bought myself a chord book, learned all the seventh chords in the book, and wrote my first song.

It felt quite natural. I never really focused — it just happened. The following year I was doing bar chords. But I really enjoyed writing that song. I used to write a diary, and I remember thinking, *this is really great — I can say stuff, without saying it directly to people. I can sing about stuff and get messages across; it's quite therapeutic.* And I just started writing songs.

My mum sent me out to go busking in town, even though I must have been absolutely terrible. But she wanted me to get out of the house and earn some money. And both my parents have written songs. One of the reasons I started writing songs, as well, is that I assumed that everybody wrote their own songs. I thought, oh, the Beatles, they write their own songs, you know, or, the Rolling Stones write their songs. I thought that's what artists did. And my granddad wrote a book of songs, in a prisoner of war camp when he was in Russia – he was captive for five years. He used to sing a bit on the French radio. He was a good singer, and a great whistler. And then my mum was really into writing songs. She used to sit at the back of class – she failed a year at school because she was so busy writing songs. She went to a competition – I suppose like an old version of The X Factor, but it wasn't on TV. And she went, and she won it. But they only wanted her songs, not her, because my mum wasn't stereotypically beautiful enough, not like more famous singers, so she refused, because she knew why they didn't want her.

So yeah – in my family, my French family, they've always written songs. I just thought it was natural. But I was never told that you could be a pop star or a rock star, never pushed in that direction. I just started writing because I really enjoyed it, and then I realized it was a way of forming an identity. I felt different, because I was in a band; I used to love carrying my guitar around, that was my look. Now I hate carrying my guitar around – maybe it's because it's become a job, you know. It's like carrying a laptop around.

MW: **What was it like at the beginning?**

JUJU: Well, I didn't really know what I wanted to do. I went to university, and studied exercise science and psychology – nothing to do with music. I took my guitar with me and I wrote some songs, and played at the local pub, at folk nights, which was far more about pulling and getting hammered. Then I didn't know what I wanted to do, and I didn't really do much music. I moved to London, got some jobs – worked as a waitress, in a t-shirt shop, all those things. Had a lot of fun. And then – I didn't actually start Little Fish until I was 26. Quite late. I suppose – I don't know. I really needed to do something with my life. And for some reason I decided then that I was going to form a band, and that was what I wanted to do. I'd been ill a bit before that, lost my voice, there were quite a lot of things – but there was basically that big pressure, a big pressure to get signed. I'd moved back to my parents' house and I was signing on, so I wasn't earning any money, and the future wasn't very bright.

My parents, at the start, weren't hugely supportive. They wanted me to do psychology or something. But when they saw that I was working really hard, getting the band together, and how much work is required to do that … it was full-time. More than full-time. So they started to support me. But I think that was one of the biggest pressures. It took me three years to get signed, and that's quite quick, from not being in loads of bands before, being quite behind, not really having any music background. I didn't know anybody in the music world. I started on Myspace, you know. I think the pressure was that I had to make it work. If not, I was gonna go and work in Tesco. And I wanted to get out of my parents' house. Although they were supportive, I couldn't stay there forever. And I didn't want to. So I had to get out – that was my only way. I suppose it was quite an old school way of thinking – that I had to get a record deal.

MW: There are very different ways of approaching a career as a musician, and there are plenty of people who don't put themselves in that position of *needing it* in the way that you describe: they do something else, and then they do the music on the side, and then if they get signed great, or if they write a "hit", that's great, but it's not necessary because they have this other life. It's like they've got this split personality. It's the same with writers, you know. Paul Auster writes about that a little in *Hand to Mouth* – "most writers lead double lives". So it's interesting that you chose not to do that. You dove into it completely.

JUJU: It's really funny actually, because I realize now that I lacked quite a lot of confidence. At university, when I did psychology, I got a first, I did quite well, but I never assumed that anybody would want to hire me. I had a real thing about *how am I gonna get a job?* I never actually knew: how do you get a job? No one tells you; people assume you know. Even careers advisors – it was all very wishy washy, very vague.

But the pivotal moment, and I must be honest, it's a really weird thing, was that when I was signing on they sent me on a course. And the course was on how to write a CV, how to get a job. It was like a week, sitting there with people who were just bored out of their minds. But actually, it was really useful. I learned: *that's how you go about doing things!*

So after that week, I kind of applied that CV knowledge to getting the band together. The first thing I did is I went to the music shops, I got all the magazines, you know, and that's how I got the gigs. We made a bit of artwork, did the demo with Nez, who I'd started to do some stuff with a bit before that, and basically I did exactly as you would if you were trying to get a job. I sent out all the CDs, with a biography and a photo, to all the pubs in London, and waited three months until we got our first gig, which was like a crappy support slot, first on, you know, at 6:30 or 7, playing to one man and his dog.

And I basically just worked up, from nothing. I didn't have that sense of logic when I finished uni – I was a bit lost, I didn't really know what to do. I probably was a bit behind in that sense. So it was quite a revelation: *oh, that's how you get a job, right, okay!* You know. *That's how you get a band together.* I just kind of applied it. It was good; in a way it worked. But it was certainly not through knowing anybody or having an in. I didn't know the business at all.

MW: **Why do you write and perform now?**

JUJU: [Laughs] It's too late! I'm too late, I've gone too far down that road! No, I dunno. Part of me loves it and part of me hates it now. I loved it until I got signed. And then there was a pressure. I used to just really enjoy writing. Now it's a lot harder to write, because it's hard to get rid of that industry pressure, where everybody's waiting for a radio song, or you get judged because people know your songs a bit more, and they can say *oh, that's not as good as the last one*, you know. That's really hard to get over unless you really don't give a fuck.

MW: **So when you write songs, is it a purely artistic compulsion, or do you have that voice in your head, saying "oh, this needs to be commercial"? Do you have a sense of what's viable and what's not?**

JUJU: When I don't is when I write the best stuff. When I do, I don't enjoy myself. I don't enjoy sitting there, I don't find it very creative, I just find it really nullifying. But that's only developed in the last few years, since the pressure's been on. Little Fish didn't get much radio play, which was the big killer. And so you can't help but think, *oh, I need to write a radio song*. But then, if I've never written a radio song, why would I start now? You know? And then, recently, getting the new stuff together, I decided not to care about anybody or what they thought. And actually I've really enjoyed writing again.

But some people are really kind of — intellectual writers. They're clever, they've been like that for years, they know music, and they write kind of — mathematically. Whereas I'm really emotional. I'm only able to write when I feel like it. Having said that, when we did the record I was put under a lot of pressure to write songs there and then by Linda [Perry]. And I did manage it. So maybe having a deadline is good.

MW: **What's your idea of "success" — both personally and for the band?**

JUJU: You know, it's a really funny thing. When I started Little Fish, I never thought beyond the first album. I thought, *if I can just fool everybody, get signed, and do a record, that would be really funny.* I never really thought beyond that. And in a way it's kind of my fault, because I do really believe that your vision is where you're gonna head. And that was as far as my vision went. Honestly, I kind of felt like I was an impostor. You know you get those people who've been musicians all their life, who fell in love with music when they were three years old and just picked it up — that's not me. So in a way I achieved what I wanted to achieve, and now I'm kind of free falling. I've found it quite hard to create another vision for what I want. Because music is important to me, and I really enjoy it when I'm doing it, but it's not *everything* that I enjoy.

So in terms of success, we achieved what I wanted [with the first album]. But now, having done that, I'd like to do a second record that I really like. Because with the first one, I think I achieved 50% of what I wanted to achieve in terms of liking it. I'd be really happy if we made a record that I really liked. And that's from having learned and experienced everything that we experienced. So that's where I'm headed, and I'm really enjoying the new music that we're doing.

I think if you like what you do and nobody else likes it, that's fine. But if you do something that you don't really like, and not everybody really likes it, then you're pissed off. So I just want to do something I really like, because then people can take it or leave it, and I couldn't care less. But I haven't quite achieved that yet. So — maybe I should have put that into the first equation: make one record, the first record, one you really like. I really admire these young kids that are coming up, these new bands — or not even new bands, but other bands — I really admire that they have a real sense of direction.

MW: That's something else I wanted to talk about. On the one hand, you're still young yourself. On the other hand, you've been doing this for a while now – seven years?

JUJU: Yeah – if I'd started when I was 20, I would've been fine. I just have a lot to catch up on!

MW: And like you say, you get these younger, newer acts coming out all the time. Do you feel like it's got harder or easier for you as time has gone on?

JUJU: I don't know. It's got easier since meeting Ben, because I have somebody that I can work with. Even before, in the old Little Fish, when he first joined, he wasn't part of the creative process because it was all done already. And Nez was never really creative in that way – he was a drummer, that was as far as it went. Ben and I have started to work together for the first time on this album; we've started to write together. And he's like the opposite of me, so that's really good. He can make what I'm thinking real. Whereas I can't. He knows what chord goes, and he also has the taste that I like. We can direct each other. I have the out-there ideas that he can make work, because he's a bit out-there but also has the skill. So yeah, in a way it's getting easier. I don't know. I think our music will definitely change, because you get older, and right now I'm not interested in shouting, or being all punky rock'n'roll.

MW: So how would you characterize the music that Little Fish has played in the past? And how would you describe what you're writing now?

JUJU: [Laughs]. Ah ... it's kind of like the yin and the yang. Before, I felt quite intense. I felt very high energy, almost quite abrasive. I wanted to be in people's faces. I wanted to shout at people, shake them up, and go beyond myself as a performer. And I do that naturally – in fact I did that in China more than I thought I was going to, because I needed to engage people. But now I kind of want to do the opposite. I just want to stand on stage, sing really softly, do slight pop songs ... I dunno, I just kind of want to play one string. I don't want to play chords. I just want to hit the same string, just one note. I'm swinging in completely the other direction now. And also things like not having Nez in the band. His drumming was very unique. Not having that has been really liberating for me. Because I realize now, and again I didn't know before, how much of an influence a drummer has in a band. Drummers – their style makes all the difference. We'd spend hours getting a snare sound in LA – and I'd be so bored, I'd just be like, *really?* Now I understand why, although we're doing the opposite now; we have one tatty snare in the garage, and we just play. That's our sound.

MW: **Are there any particular themes or thoughts that you find your-self returning to in your songs?**

JUJU: I think my songs are quite depressing overall. But I've been trying to make them less depressing recently [Laughs]. Yeah. I used to be quite angry, and depressive. But I don't feel so angry and depressed anymore. So I'm kind of more relaxed, more fun. But there's quite a lot of loneliness probably, themes of loneliness. I'm generally quite philosophical.

MW: **Would you consider yourself a private person? How much of yourself do you feel comfortable revealing in your music?**

JUJU: I'm good at deflecting. I don't put everything into songs. But I probably sing a lot of the songs with the emotion that I feel about them. I don't write many direct love songs. I like to write in the third person. Some stuff hits a nerve, more than others. But I'm quite good at hiding a little bit. You can use metaphors – I really like that.

MW: **How would you describe your relationship with your fans?**

JUJU: I'm always really surprised that we have fans. I'm always really appreciative. I think because it was such hard work to even get any-where, I've always appreciated any support. And I just think it's human decency to appreciate people, and to care about them. They care about us, I care about them. I really do.

MW: **What about your relationship to other people – band members, producers, musicians, whoever?**

JUJU: I think people probably assume that I'm a lot more confident with my writing. I think people always assume that I knew what I want-ed, or knew what I was doing. But I had no clue. I had no idea who

Linda Perry was; I didn't even want to know really, because I didn't – I dunno, I didn't even know that you had different producers for different records.

MW: **Do you think that helped you, in a way? Because you didn't have these preconceived notions of things and these expectations, you were able to …**

JUJU: Naïvely just jump into things! Yeah, I think it went for me and against me. I think it really helped Little Fish get signed and go around the world and do all these things, because if I had known what I know now, I would have been a lot more negative. I probably would have thought it could never happen, and probably would have held myself back. So it gave me freedom to think that I could do this. But that's what I admire in the kids these days – they seem to know so much, they know how the industry works, they know who they should be working with, they know where to play, they know what's cool, they know what's hip. I had no idea. No idea. So there you go: I'm amazed at these kids – kids, I say kids – these young people who are producing music light years beyond what I was doing at their age.

MW: **Are there any particular artists that inspire or move you?**

JUJU: I used to be quite inspired by PJ Harvey and Patti Smith. Those two always went together, because they were strong: the strong women of music. They sang music that I really liked. And Patti Smith's lyrics were always really poetic and clever. It used to be my kind of check on lyrics: *would Patti Smith approve?* And I had a picture of her on my desk, and if I thought *yeah*, it would get the go-ahead; if it was a no, it would be dumped. But having met her a few times – I kind of realize that I was a bit disappointed. So I don't really have that anymore. I still love her music and that's great, but I think that iconic thing has kind of melted a little bit.

MW: **It's a delicate balance to strike, with idols: do you want to meet them? Do you want to just leave them as they are? Do you want to develop a relationship with them? It can go either way – it could be a really good thing for some people, but also, like you say, it can be disappointing. And you're in the same position – there are people who listen to Little Fish who look up to you.**

JUJU: Yeah! And I'm sure we let people down – but inadvertently.

MW: **Right. You can't be anybody other than who you are.**

JUJU: I think people don't like change. As we've changed over the years we've lost some people. We gained other people. But you have to, like a child grows up. And I think that's always a bit sensitive for some people. Starting out as a two-piece, becoming at three-piece, now losing part of a piece, adding other pieces.

MW: **But I think that's a very natural thing to do. Like you say, it's like growing up, it's just what happens, people change. And you do get bands who sound exactly the same, time and time again, which can be really boring.**

JUJU: It's a recipe for sound. Like the hit recipe.

MW: **And it's great that it works for them financially, but I don't necessarily want to hear the same thing over and over and over again.**

JUJU: I don't know how they do that. I'm the sort of person who hates to walk the same street twice. I will purposely go up one street and then go around a whole different way to come back. Or walk on the other side at least. I can't bear doing the same thing twice. So: not very good at putting in a box.

MW: **Do you think making good music is an end in itself, or a means to an end?**

JUJU: I really want to do a record that I really like, because I'd love to take it out on tour. I'd like people to hear it, but I'd like to tour it, travel it. One thing I really do like is performing on stage. It's when I feel the most free. I really enjoy it, I have a lot of fun. So I think it's kind of a means to an end. I believe that if you make an album that's liked, or that you like, you can work with it. I've got nothing against being famous and nothing against making money. You have to make money to pay your rent, to live. But I think I won't do it at the cost of sacrificing things – like writing music that I don't like. I won't put that first. I'll put the music that I like before making money or becoming famous. That probably holds me back in some ways. I think people probably assume that

I want to be famous. Well, I don't know what people think. But they're wrong. I'm quite happy doing what I'm doing. I do like touring. I hope we can tour our next record. So I hope it's good enough to attract some sort of attention. You know, you need people to play in front of. It's kind of like a rolling stone, a vicious circle.

MW: **What's the hardest part of being a musician?**

JUJU: The hardest bit? The waiting. Waiting. Waiting for things to get done, finished. Waiting for people to answer emails. Waiting to hear back from people. That's probably the hardest bit. Even I'm slow, though.

MW: **What keeps you afloat if you're having a rough time?**

JUJU: Swimming [Laughs]. I think there's an inner drive. You've got this instinctive – fire, drive, whatever. You can't put it out. Even on a bad day, it dims or smokes even, but it still comes back. I mean, what do you call it? A sort of – a creative thing inside you.

MW: **What's the most rewarding part of being a musician?**

JUJU: [Laughs] I was gonna say a paycheque, but … pfffft. Um, most rewarding? I dunno. It's kind of funny, because you do all that work – and I think some people get really excited by the things that might obviously be the most rewarding, like touring with Blondie or Courtney Love or something. But actually that's just stuff you can say to people so that people will take you a bit more seriously – like speaking a language that they understand.

I think one one of the most rewarding moments I've ever had happened quite recently, in Beijing. We played this show for a festival. And I was just really enjoying feeling free, the freest I've ever felt on stage, with Ben and Mike, who's drumming with us at the moment. We were just improvising stuff for the audience, and changing stuff live, and that's the first time that that's ever happened.

But I don't know. I don't know what the most rewarding part is. I'm really enjoying the new stuff that we're recording. That's quite reward-ing because we're doing it ourselves. It's really odd – I can't answer this question. You'd think getting signed – well, getting signed was really great, because I could tell my parents, and doing a record was kind of the thing that was expected. But it wasn't necessarily the most rewarding.

I think my favourite moment is when I've finished writing a song, and I really like it. That's probably the biggest reward. It soon goes. That feeling lasts a day, maybe two. And then you've gotta write another one. So I think that's probably one of the most rewarding moments. And when you're recording in the garage, and it's going well, that's quite fun. It's very surprising. You know, when you've tied two pieces of wood to something, when you do random stuff and it works, that's good. I think they're the most rewarding moments, for me.

MW: **Yeah – the way you've set things up now, playing in the garage, doing things in that sort of DIY way, borrowing violins, is interesting. Do you want to sound like you've recorded in your garage – is it an aesthetic that appeals to you, or just a necessity?**

JUJU: It's all part of doing the opposite of everything that Little Fish has ever done – getting away from that big LA studio. I'm not that person, I'll never be tidy or neat or perfect. So why go into a perfect environment?

But it's kind of two things: one, yes, I want to do it, and two, I also have to do it. Because there is no other way. I don't feel the need to run around and get a record deal. I just want to do something I like. And I quite like the idea of having limits: like, we don't have any cymbals, therefore, we won't have any cymbals. Or, we don't own this, so we won't use that. I want to make do with what we've got, but the real way – I don't want to be in a Dave Grohl garage. I bet his garage is nothing like our garage. No, we're recording in a *garage*. Like yeah, we have two microphones that aren't even recording mics. And we don't really know where we're gonna put them.

So I dunno, I think it has even more of that punk ethic than Little Fish has ever had – it's how things should have been in the first place basically. But we can put our ideas out there and see what works – we don't have a big record deal. Producers, big studios, they cost a lot of money. And we don't have that money. So yeah. It's out of necessity, but I'm really happy to do it. And actually I'm really enjoying it. It's nice to have control.

MW: **Speaking of control … I want to ask you about your experience with and relationship to the inverted commas version of the "music** industry", or the "record business", or whatever you want to call it. I know that experiences differ, and the experience you had being signed is going to be different from other people's, but it's an important part of Little Fish's history.

JUJU: I think the whole industry feeds off people being neurotic and needy. It preys on people's weaknesses and desires.

MW: I guess that's the only way it works: you have to want something, you have to have some dream for them ...

JUJU: For them to capitalize on and exploit. So yeah, on that level, I'd say that's the bad side, isn't it. I just think the industry tends to attract [vulnerable] people. It tends to exploit those people [...] It sells you a dream – it's a bit like the American dream. It's a good sales pitch. And I believed it. I wholly believed it.

MW: **There's no reason not to. It does happen for some people.**

JUJU: Well, you're told that, yeah.

MW: **And there are people who've made millions of dollars on their own songs. But not very many. And the things they've had to give up to do that are probably pretty big.**

JUJU: I'm not sure it makes people happy, either.

MW: **Right. I guess to want that, to have that dream, you have to be a bit obsessive.**

JUJU: You have to have a big hole in your personality. Maybe I had a big hole. Probably. But I don't think it was that big. I didn't really know what I was doing.

MW: **You mentioned feeling free earlier. Does the experience a band has with the record business depend to a certain extent on how much they're willing to give up? I mean, if you are a really good musician, and you get lucky, and you're working with people that want the same things that you want, then that's great. But did you ever find,** when you were signed, that there were things that you couldn't do that you wanted to do?

JUJU: Well, we were unfortunate. I suppose our label wasn't really "on it". It took two years before our record even got released. That was really demoralizing. We had to sit in limbo, and that really deflated us as people. The hype that we'd spend those years building was – a lot happens in two years. So yeah, that wasn't so good.

MW: So would you be happy to be signed again, if you got offered a deal? Obviously it would have to be the right deal, but ...

JUJU: That's a really interesting thing. Because it can be really good. It can help you. I think it helps people who are lucky, who are signed to the right label. I think we made a bad decision. We made a good decision, but also a bad decision.

MW: Is there any way you think you could have known, though, whether or not it was going to be right?

JUJU: No. It's pot luck. There's a lot of bullshit in this industry. And I think it's quite dangerous for young people. I mean, again, I've met quite a lot of younger bands who just don't want to get signed. They seem to know a lot more than I knew. And it may be that the information's more out there. Or you've just got to be more willing to play the bullshit game. Maybe I'm not so willing. I'm not so easy to manipulate. I think young people have to be a bit careful. Because they can be easily bedazzled. I think we were a bit bedazzled.

MW: Especially if that's what you've been working for: you've been working to be signed.

JUJU: ... And then someone shows you interest. It's amazing. Someone takes notice of you! Yeah, it's quite flattering, I suppose [...] I suppose the kind of positive side is that if you haven't got any money – it's a business, isn't it. And if you're – let's just say, for example, you're a really good musician, you make great music, it's a structure that will help you make it your living. That's why anybody wants to get signed.

MW: So can you talk a little more about the positive experience of being signed, about how it actually helped Little Fish?

JUJU: Well, it was a relief, because that was what we'd aimed for, that was the target. It's like seeing the top of one mountain; and when we got to the top of the mountain, we realized there were loads more mountains, but we were happy just to get to the top of that mountain, because we thought then the label would help us climb all the other mountains. That was fine. It gives you status, if you get signed to a major label. People seem to change. They give you a different kind of respect, which may sound really silly, but it's true. All of the sudden, Little Fish was worth more.

[...]

Being signed – it does a lot of good. It creates excitement around the band, it gives people that confidence, that "dream might come true" feeling. And it did a lot of good things [for us]. I just want to clarify that being independent is great, but being signed can also be really good. I think you're lucky if you come out unscathed and you're lucky if you make money and you're lucky if you get the record you want and you're lucky if you get on the radio and you're lucky if you get all the press and the festivals – you're probably also really talented, but you're pretty lucky. Because for all that to line-up – and all it takes is your A&R man to be sacked or leave the company for you to be screwed, you know. No one's gonna work your record. So it's a bit of luck and talent and hard work, but I just wanted to say that. I wouldn't have that nice guitar I'm playing if we hadn't been signed. Ben wouldn't have had the Hammond. I wouldn't have had half the clothes I wear, quite frankly. And I wouldn't have been able to have some money and be relaxed for a little bit. So yeah – it can be great. It's just, like everything, there's always another side.

MW: Do you think things are changing, that independent artists can have that same kind of status?

JUJU: I don't know. It's interesting. It would be nice to think that it might level out. I think people respect independent artists. But I still think that there's a status thing about being signed to a major label. And the positives – we got some money, you know, an advance, that meant that I could stop scrounging off my parents and be self-sufficient, which was amazing.

MW: **What are the terms with something like that? Do you then owe the label that advance?**

JUJU: It's purely on the record sales — unless, nowadays they sign 360 deals. We had half a 360 deal — it was more like, if we sold over x amount of merch we would have to give a percentage of that profit to the company. But we never sold beyond that ridiculous amount of merch.

MW: **So it's kind of like a student loan, where if you start earning above a certain threshold you have to start paying it back.**

JUJU: Yeah, I suppose so. On the merch side of things. On the record side of things, it was if you sell x amount of records, you have to pay; in fact you have to pay all the money back, and it's only after you've paid the money back that you start to get a share of the profits.

We have never seen a balance sheet, so I have no idea how much they spent on us and I have no idea how much we've sold. All I know is that we sold out of our records, in the shops. They printed 5,000. It was only in the UK. And now I think they're quite hard to find — maybe a few charity shops. A collector's item!

The record company also pay for radio, they pay for press. They pay out of your money that you're signed — so we had a budget that the label gave us. We never saw any of that money, but we didn't have to pay [i.e. to have their record made]. Some people do. It depends on your advance. And that can be quite a lot of money — really expensive. A big producer is really expensive. Mastering a record is really expensive. We're talking, you know, it could be up to a hundred thousand pounds to make a major label record. Easily.

So it gave us some status. And people are fickle like that, people are silly — we weren't any different than we were before. We weren't any better, or worse — well, we got better over the years, but we weren't radically different, I was still myself and Nez was still himself. But when you get signed, all of the sudden it's different. And you get flown around to different places, you know. And that's the thing — it's much easier to get on bigger tours, it's much easier to book bigger tours if you have radio play, and you're more likely to have radio play if you can pay for great press and radio pluggers. So that was all brilliant. That was the kind of plan you're sold, that's the dream you're sold. But in practice – when you've got people working for you and working on other records, you might not be the priority. Which means you might not really get any of that.

MW: **Did you feel like you got to work with the kind of producers and people you would have wanted to work with?**

JUJU: We didn't have any choice. We had to do the record with Linda Perry. Had I known what I know now – but I was really naïve, and didn't even know anything about producers – I wouldn't have made the record in America, and I wouldn't have worked with Linda Perry. Although – and this is really important to say – I really respect that she was the one who gave us that opportunity. She put her money where her mouth was and invested in us.

MW: **So you've been able to live on some of the money that you got from that deal?**

JUJU: Not only that – what happened was that you then have this record, and whether it's big or not, you've got Universal at the bottom of it, which means people take more notice of it, which means we were able to – you know, Rock Band came to see us play in America, and they then decided to take three of our tracks and put them on their computer game, which, you know, publishing money. And also Tony Hawk [*Tony Hawk's Pro Skater*], and then a movie with Hillary Swank. Which unfortunately wasn't a huge hit! If only it had been, but it wasn't. It was *The Resident*. Yeah. So that was amazing.

MW: **So that's where the money is.**

JUJU: Yeah. That's why everybody wants their song in an advert. To recoup on the record sale you've gotta sell a lot of records. If you want to make the money, keep hold of your publishing and get in a film or an advert or a computer game. That's where the money is. So I didn't ever really care if we recouped or not on the record. Because I knew it was ridiculous. We'd got more out of them in that sense, because we got a record, a bit of status, we got instruments, free guitars, Ben got a Hammond organ and Nez got a drum kit. It was great. It was just the fact that they didn't release our record for two years. That's pretty stressful. That means you're just waiting around and all the buzz you've built up for yourself dies and everybody forgets you and it's all a bit of an anticlimax. So that was shit. And a waste, you know. And they own the record, as well.

MW: **What was their rationale for waiting?**

JUJU: It was just pure incompetence. Really bad organization on their part.

MW: **Because they own the record, does that mean you can't use the music?**

JUJU: We can use the music – you have to have permission to use the recordings. You can't re-record the songs within like 15 years. They technically own it all in that sense. But if you're lucky and you've got a strong manager, you could maybe get the record back, which happens. And then re-release it in territories it hasn't been released in. It's only been released in England! Universal – in the US, they didn't even release it there. Or in Europe, or anywhere. They promised us a lot and really didn't deliver. But by the time they took two years to release it, it was just like … I was already destroyed. And even when they did, it was all, "by the way, tomorrow we're releasing your record!" It's like, thanks for telling me! The advert on YouTube – I made that. I did what I could do. But it's just complete bullshit, you know. They don't care, they've got loads of money to waste, it seems. They screw people's lives up. Oh well. We carry on.

MW: **What was the process of recording like? You were flown out to LA to do that. Did it happen over a fairly short period of time?**

JUJU: We essentially recorded the album in two weeks. And then there were a few tracks that I didn't like, and we got flown out there again to do a few more tracks. A lot of it was written on the day it was recorded in the end – so *Bang Bang, You, Me & the TV, Luck's Run Out, Sorry State*, I can't remember – I think there's another track. They were all written in the morning. I had to write them in the morning and then we'd record them in the day. It was a long process – I'd write the song, then they would spend like most of the day getting a drum sound, and then we'd do three or four takes of the song, and if it wasn't good enough, we didn't do the song.

MW: So were there some that got thrown out?

Juju: Yeah. It was really harsh actually. I didn't enjoy the process, and Linda was really hard. We'd never done any recording before – we'd done a few demos, one demo really, and I didn't know what it was like to record a record. Nobody explained it.

MW: Do you think it sounds better for having had the support of the label?

JUJU: No, not necessarily. I think it probably would have been better if we'd recorded it rough in our garage, because that's the kind of band we were [...] I kind of always knew in the back of my mind that *Baffled and Beat* wasn't the record that was going to blow people apart. I'm not even sure that I could ever make that record. You realize that there are a lot of talented people out there. And also, again, what is success? You know, like Adele, at the moment, is the biggest thing, the hottest seller, but quite frankly, I could really live without her.

MW: Well, people's tastes are very fickle. It's hard to know what's going to move them.

JUJU: I think that kind of music is for people who don't like music. People who buy two or three records a year from – what's big? Coldplay.

MW: Right. So in that case it doesn't matter if you do the same thing over and over again. But it's a different relationship.

JUJU: Radiohead kind of managed it. They've done different stuff. Although they've kind of stuck to that out-thereish stuff. They do whatever they want, but they're also a really creative band, you know, I think there's no doubt about it that they're all incredible musicians in their own rights and creative. You get bands that are actually really talented. But you also get bands who don't – who are more industry-made-up than actual creative people.

MW: I know this is something you particularly wanted to talk about – the deliberate choices you've made about Little Fish's sound over the years, the ethos behind the decisions you've made musically.

JUJU: I was really keen for Little Fish to be purist, in the sense that at the time, when we started, there were loads of bands who were getting into the technology of using click tracks live and computers and sounds. So you'd see a drummer drumming, but half the drum sound was just playback, so they were drumming along to playback. And that still happens a lot. The whole spectrum of sound you can get using lots of different pedals and – everything, reverb on the voice, you know. And I decided to very deliberately keep it really pure. I didn't want any pedals, didn't want any effects on my guitar. Straight out the amp. When we recorded there was no click track, it was all live. And there were no overdubs, so there was no re-singing of vocals, it was mostly all done live. No backing vocals. So it was all really raw, but we were in the wrong environment maybe to do a raw record. If you want to do a raw record like that, maybe don't do it in a really posh studio, because the sound doesn't really work. Not for us, anyway, it didn't. It comes out like an old polished pair of shoes. That doesn't really work: keep them old, or get a new pair. But anyway, the point is – that's why I think the record didn't sound right, because it was recorded in the wrong place.

MW: Did you find any resistance to that from anybody who had input when you were signed? Were there people trying to steer you away from that kind of sound?

JUJU: I think Linda was quite happy to go with that. But I think there's definitely a difference between American and English rock, and sounds, and that didn't work for us, and the culture didn't work – our lives didn't seem to agree, which I think is why the music got a bit lost. But some people really like that record. It's just not the one I wanted to make. So now we're doing what we probably should have done in the first place, we're making our second record in our garage. We've got two microphones. We're hoping to get a better one for the vocals, but we've started to record, and we use whatever we've got in the house, and that's the ethos. Don't try and compete with something you can't compete with. I'm not even going to bother trying to produce a huge sounding record, because we're never gonna get that sound in our garage. It's not the sound we're going for.

Having said that, it's a different sound we're going for this time – I do want harmonies, we've got another singer in the band, and I want to change the kind of drums, not big rock drums, keep it really simple, simple, not play big rock chords – do the opposite, basically, of what we did before. Minimalistic, I think. So yeah, we're very excited. It's taken awhile to find a new direction, but we're getting there. That's another thing – after all that, the two years of waiting for your record to be released, it being released, it being kind of – just not breaking the ground that you'd hoped for, and then the label and everybody not giving a fuck, you end up quite depressed. It was really hard to get back together, and Nez left the band because he didn't have any money left, and he had a kid, and all that stuff – I think he lost the will to live, musically, which was really hard. I tried to keep him in the band for another year, but we just kind of fizzled. Couldn't do it. It was quite a hard few years. But now, with a new idea, we're back on track. It's kind of soul-destroying. I admire people who can just carry on. The experience is tough, and Nez – as much as he was there, he's a busy family man. So it was basically me carrying a lot, doing a lot, and in the end I couldn't do it all, not by myself. Robert's been great, he's really supportive. It's thanks to him that Rock Band came to see us play, and got into a movie.

MW: **How did he come to be your manager?**

JUJU: Long story short – he came to see us play at a gig, and liked us. He took us after we got signed, and after we'd made the record. Which is really rare, and really hard. So we made the record without any manager. Which was another really bad idea, because we had to deal with the record company, and it was hard to be taken seriously. So it was pretty tough, not much fun. And finding a new manager is really hard when you're in that position, because what's in it for them? You've already been signed, so there's no money there.

MW: **But he was willing to take you on.**

JUJU: Yeah. I mean, I've never sold Little Fish's publishing, so we own it, which means that there's always the possibility that Robert could eventually get, if we ever got a big publishing deal, he could get some money that way. But at the same time, he's just awesome. There've been times when he could've taken money, and he just said, no, you guys need it more than me. Which is really rare. And he's just such a great guy, he's got integrity and morals.

MW: **It's nice that you've got somebody who can play the game but isn't going to sacrifice you.**

JUJU: Well also for him, two grand is nothing. But, having said that, you can still be rich and be an asshole, and take that cut. And he's never taken anything, never taken a percentage of a gig fee, never asked for us to pay back money that he's lent us [laughs] – we're gonna have a huge bill if ever we make loads of money. But for now, if we don't make any money he makes no money, and if we do, well, I'll happily pay the money that he's earned.

MW: **Does he have any input into your sound, or the decisions you're making at the moment?**

JUJU: He does. He would. But – I wrote a whole album last year that nobody liked. Well, he didn't like it, and the press people or the radio people didn't like it. They didn't think it would be a hit, there weren't any hits – this fucking hit thing. Which was also really demoralizing. In the end, you just, after writing 20 new songs, you just go, I can't write anything that makes anybody happy, so what the fuck am I doing? So that was a bit demoralizing as well last year.

So this year I've decided to start writing this new record, and I'm not playing any of it to him, and when it's done I'll say, here it is, and if he likes it, that will be great. And if he doesn't like it, as long as it's something I'm really happy with, I believe in it, I will take that record myself to the people and speak to them. Because I realize that you're the artist, the manager isn't the artist. You're lucky if you've got that relationship, but I realize that we don't quite correlate artistically, not fully. He works on a hit thing – he's not into the alternative. In that way we don't really work as a management–artist team. But he's been so loyal to us, and so nice, and he's still there for us. I just think it's more important. I wouldn't want to jump ship. Although I have sent him a track recently, because I knew he'd like it, because everybody says it's a radio song – which he really liked – Melt Into the Sun.

MW: **So you might have a hit on your hands...**

JUJU: Wouldn't that be funny! Well, I don't think we'll ever have a major hit. But we could have an indie hit. Major hits, you've gotta compete with the Rihannas of the world, the Jay Zs – forget it. America's listening to R'n'B, or big synth pop, or, I dunno, Jessie J – that's "hit" music. That's not Little Fish. So we're never gonna have that. But what would be nice is to be able to give people the opportunity to actually hear us, and have a fan base so we can do gigs and tour. That's the aim really.

So yeah, I'd never complain about having a mini hit, but the likelihood is pretty small. And that's fine. I'm kind of happier. I mean, I had that option at the beginning of the year, you know, Robert was like, "okay, so we're gonna send you out to Nashville or New York to work with these songwriters and then we're gonna get this huge producer to work with you and then we'll have a hit record". And I was like, that's not me. I don't want to go and be in America and write songs that I don't like and then sing songs with a band I don't even know – why would I want to do that? That's not me. So, sorry Robert. If you want to do that, do it with a young 20-year-old who's happy to do it. I think it's too late. I think I'm too strong-minded now and know what I like, and know what I want to do. I'm happy with that. He's got other artists he can do that with. I think he's getting to know me. But I think he just thinks, "Jules does her thing. And when she's ready, I'll be there". Which is really cool. You sometimes wish you had that hip young trendy manager who's gonna get everything you do, and be there, and work really hard every minute of the day. Well, if you find that person, you're really lucky. Good luck.

It's like everything. You compromise. I'm sure he compromises with us. He's got nothing to lose. If we stay, he doesn't lose anything by waiting around, because he's got enough other things to do. We're not asking for any money at the moment, because we're trying to do it all ourselves. The less you ask anybody the less input they can have and the less you owe them. So my philosophy with this record is just to do as much of it as we can ourselves, and don't ask for anything, because then you don't owe anybody anything. Which is why we're doing it in our garage and we've only got two mics and no cymbals. It's fine. We've got pots and pans. So we'll see. It's nice to give yourself boundaries sometimes as well.

MW: Yeah. It's great to have control over what you do, but it can also be really intimidating, to sit down with a blank page. You have so many choices that you often can't start. It's almost like a game – if you give yourself limits it becomes easier to actually create something. Otherwise you could theoretically make anything.

JUJU: Yeah. If you've got bananas and a bit of flour you're gonna make banana cake. If you've got like, bananas, peaches, strawberries, raspberries, and whatever, and chocolate – you're gonna fuck that cake up. It's not gonna taste of much, really. Mush. Unless you've got a great producer – again, like, if we had the option to have a really great producer, someone we really wanted to work with, which, there are a few people – we would do it. So it's not that we're against having lots of money and choosing. But right now we don't have that luxury. So forget it. So it's not 100% our choice – it's like 50/50, half choice, half necessity.

MW: What do you do on a day-to-day basis? What's a typical sort of work day as a musician?

JUJU: [Laughs] Work day? Oh god, they're so different. Let's pretend it's a day where we're recording or something.

MW: Well, I'm interested in that – I'm interested in a day where you're doing something like recording. But I'm also interested in the really mundane stuff that you have to do, you know, the emails and stuff.

JUJU: Well, I do less now. That's another thing that happens: you get signed and all of the sudden you don't have to book your own gigs, you don't have to talk to anybody. You've got people doing this and people doing that – if you're lucky, if they're doing what they say they're doing. Most of the time they're not, which means you're sitting around waiting for people to do something that you know you could do better. But once you get signed, once you've gone through all that, you don't have to do it, so your job is basically to be ready to sing at all times. You have to keep your voice in good shape, or write, or prepare for a gig, band practice. Those are the kind of normal things you'd do.

But on a daily basis, now? God. I get up. And I have breakfast. And I go to my computer and I check my emails [laughs] ... it's really boring. And then, depending on what's going on, I might get inspired by some-

thing and write a blog post, or I might not, and I might just go to the
swimming pool. It's quite important to keep fit, actually. For me anyway. Performing, touring, breathing – I've got asthma as well, so I have
to keep my lungs moving. And then I'll come back and have lunch. And
then I might think about writing. And I'll just go to my desk and sit
there. And probably be distracted by Facebook for a little bit. And then
maybe think about picking up the guitar. And I'll stare at the guitar for
a bit. And then I'll pick it up. And then I'll just sit there and strum. I
mean, I don't even do this every day. So, you know. And then I sit and
just strum. Or just kind of – write a line. I could, in a day, just write one
line, and that's it.

MW: I sometimes feel like I should be able to do more. I spend so
much of my day not writing; so to write 500 words in a day – I should
be able to write ten times that. But do you ever feel like actually all of
that space around the action – even if all you do is write a line – do
you feel like some of the process of writing a song isn't actually the
writing?

JUJU: Well, Ben's convinced that it is, which is why he lets me get
away with it.

MW: Yeah, I've convinced myself that it is as well. But I don't know.

JUJU: I don't think I've got quite there yet. I still think I'm just procras-
tinating. I used to sit there for hours, I was far more productive, I'd
write a lot more songs. But once I've finally managed to get myself to
the desk, I will write something, be it a poem, or a little thing, or a
song. I mean, yesterday I outlined two new songs, in the space of about
an hour. Just because I was so bored, and I wanted to leave the desk as
soon as I could. Sometimes you've just got to do it quickly, and then
leave it, and then come back to it. *Am I Crazy?* took me probably about – I
don't know – how many years? About eight years to write. I started it
when I was about 18, and I finished it when I was about 26, 27. I never
quite finished it. *Darling Dear* I wrote in like 20 minutes, from beginning
to end.

So – I just don't know. As long as I write a little bit every day – not
even every day, because I don't write every day. As long as I write a little
bit occasionally, I mean, most weekdays, I know that I'm going to piece
something together. I suppose I've learned that about myself. I know I'll

piece a song together. It goes back to that thing: before, I felt a lot more pressure to do music. Now, my life's slightly different. God, I sound really – I don't have that same drive. I don't have the same pressure. I feel a bit beaten by the whole process; it did beat me for a bit. I felt a bit – depressed, kind of disillusioned, by the whole industry. I didn't feel that I wanted to be part of it again. And now I feel like I'm ready – I feel like I'm back to just doing music again, rather than being part of an industry. Because I don't really care about the industry. You know. I feel like I'll cross that bridge when I come to it. Right now I'm just in creative mode. It's quite nice. You have to be able to brush the shit off your shoulders, escape the pressures.

But yeah. That's what I do. I just do my day. I go swimming, I come back, I sit at my desk, try and write a song, sometimes it happens, sometimes it doesn't, and if it doesn't, I'll get really annoyed, and I'll be really pissed off, and I'll feel really shit, so I'll either carry on – like I might sit there for three or four hours until finally something comes – or, I'll get upset and I'll just come back again tomorrow and try again. But I reckon that's probably the competitive side – I don't want to lose. That's it really. It's kind of always on my mind, things are always ticking.

MW: **Right. You're never divorced from that process, are you? It's not like – anything – waitressing or something, where when you're not physically there you can't really worry about it.**

JUJU: A lot of people that I know are far more disciplined than me [...] I have spurts.

MW: **How do you decide if a song you've written is good?**

JUJU: There are some songs that sneak past me that I don't really like, that I let in anyway. But they soon drop off the wagon. I tend to just veto things as I'm doing them. Sometimes you do a song and it's not as good as you hoped or thought it was. But you have to go through that process. You really do have to write the shit before you get to the good. And yeah, it's a feeling, isn't it. You just write it and you like it. If you believe in it, it's great.

MW: **What do you hope that people get out of listening to your music?**

JUJU: I think when someone writes and says, "I'm listening to your music, it's making me feel really good" – or, "I really identify with this feeling", or ... if they get something out of it, that's really rewarding. I think that's something that I never thought about before, until more recently. I think it's quite a mature thing – I think what I'd call an "intellectual writer", somebody who writes with other people in mind, they write about a feeling that lots of people can relate to. And those probably end up being some of the hit songs, because it's kind of a – unanimous feeling, between people. I never cared about that. I always just wrote what I thought and what I felt. I wrote selfishly.

But more recently I've started to think about that sometimes, to think about the other person more. But again – I don't really write for other people, in that sense, because that's like writing for a corporation. It's got to be you, at the end of the day. And I don't like fake people, sing-ers, writers. All my favorite people are genuine artists. I dunno, I've never really thought about people actually listening to the stuff. It's quite a compliment.

MW: **Fifty years, or 100 years from now, what would you hope people would write or remember about Little Fish?**

JUJU: I don't know. I wouldn't even like to assume that we would be remembered for anything. I'd like to be – if that was the case – I'd like to be remembered for being strong, sticking to my guns, doing what I wanted to do. Because hopefully that will make people strong enough to do what they want to do, whatever it is. It doesn't have to be music. I think that's my general ethos. Be strong. And be true to yourself. I don't like people who manipulate themselves to be somebody else, in order to achieve something. I think that's something you learn over time – or you don't. Some people go the other way. So I think that's it really. Give people the belief. I think there's a lot of society that's prepared to knock you down, say that you should be different, in order to make you try and be like everybody else, conform. I admire people who are free thinkers.

MW: **If you weren't doing music and could do anything in the world, what would you do?**

JUJU: Ha. I'd be an astronaut. No – actually no, there's too much time alone. I like people. That's one thing I do enjoy. I love travelling. I like coming home, too. I don't know. I think I'd be an academic. If I could do anything, I think I'd be an academic, or a psychologist. I think the deeper you go into something — anybody who's got that insight or knowledge, if you're impassioned by that — it's got to be really interesting. Although it's probably a bit late for me to do that now! I haven't got the patience. But if I could do anything, I think it would be to be really good at something like that. I'll never be that person, though.

Outro

As the city hangs at my window I think of crawling between the sheets and trying to sleep. When I am sad and so nervous I can't sleep or so in love with someone that I can't see, I have to stop myself from pushing everything to a place where nothing matters and having read the story of Little Fish, here is one last thing that I want to tell you about; to tell you about my life and the way that it is, to remind you of yours. Everything that we did does matter and it is never too late or too early to learn something. *Je me suis cent fois perdu* and after the long journey of Little Fish, Ben and I decided to leave the band there in the ocean, under the horizon. We started a new band, Candy Says. I can't read her lips all the time but she is a free spirit. Far more free than Little Fish ever was. Candy Says is our band as of 2013. Why do this? Because I don't want to lose faith. The good life doesn't just come and knock at your door, you have to go out into the world and make it for yourself and I recognize myself for what I am and for the things that I hate. My actions ricochet. I never cease to be surprised by the day, constantly satisfying those little desires of nothing, the simple sensations of existing at all. How simple. I laugh. In bed. Out loud. At my simple thoughts. And my simple thoughts are my richness and my passion for writing and performing music sticks to me like electricity. It saves me and speaks to me straight. That is not what Little Fish now says to me, but what Candy Says.

– Juju

Endnotes

1. @britessential: "@Littlefishmusic Ok. Cool. For me @Littlefishmusic is more than just music, it represents freedom of expression and honesty, which is rare!" 12 March 2012.
2. Dorian Lynskey, "Leonard Cohen: 'All I've got to put in a song is my own experience'", *Guardian*, 19 January 2012. http://www.guardian.co.uk/music/2012/jan/19/leonard-cohen.
3. ibid.
4. Bas Grasmayar, "The answer is the ecosystem: marketing music through non-linear communication", 2011. http://bashashas.com/thesis/.
5. Bas Grasmayar, "'Why music is not a product & three reasons why that's a good thing", Techdirt, 14 February 2012. http://www.techdirt.com/articles/20120213/08223317744/why-music-is-not-product-three-reasons-why-thats-good-thing.shtml.
6. Kristin Hersh, "Eden", 26 January 2012. http://www.kristinhersh.com/eden/.
7. Geoff Dyer, *Out of Sheer Rage*, pp.147–9.
8. Sophie Ratcliffe (ed), *P.G.Wodehouse: A Life in Letters*, p.238, p.519.
9. Steve Lawson, "Independent music manifesto", 16 September 2009. http://www.stevelawson.net/2009/09/independent-music-manifesto/.
10. Derk Sivers, "Seth Godin on spreading music and selling intimacy", 25 January 2010. http://sivers.org/seth-godin.
11. Andrew Dubber, *Music in the Digital Age*. https://leanpub.com/dubber.
12. http://www.lettersofnote.com/2012/03/you-are-mistaken-in-calling-it-novel.html.
13. Kristin Hersh, "Eden", 26 January 2012. http://www.kristinhersh.com/eden/.

14. http://www.kickstarter.com/projects/amandapalmer/amanda-palmer-the-new-record-art-book-and-tour.
15. Steve Lawson, "Every artist is a Kickstarter project", 14 February 2012. http://www.stevelawson.net/2012/02/every-artist-is-a-kickstarter-project/#more-2890.
16. Ian Bogost, "Kickstarter: crowdfunding platform or reality show?", Fast Company, 18 July 2012. http://www.fastcompany.com/1843007/kickstarter-fundraising-or-a-new-kind-of-entertainment.
17. Sam Jones, "UK music sales decline for seventh successive year despite downloads", Guardian, 2 January 2012. http://www.guardian.co.uk/music/2012/jan/02/uk-music-sales-decline-2011.
18. By 26.6% in 2011. (Sam Jones, "UK music sales decline for seventh successive year despite downloads", Guardian, 2 January 2012. http://www.guardian.co.uk/music/2012/jan/02/uk-music-sales-decline-2011.)
19. Quote by Liverpool-based music writer Peter Guy. See Alexandra Topping, "Young musicians attract fan funding to avoid reliance on record industry", Guardian, 29 April 2012. http://www.guardian.co.uk/music/2012/apr/29/young-musicians-fan-funding-record-industry?CMP=twt_fd.
20. Louis Barabbas, "Musicians exposing themselves in public", 12 July 2012. http://louisbarabbas.com/articles/musicians-exposing-themselves-in-public/.
21. Michael Raisanen, "The current rage in branding: fake authenticity is now a-okay", Fast Company, 15 March 2012. http://www.fastcodesign.com/1669220/the-current-rage-in-branding-fake-authenticity-is-now-a-okay.
22. Alexandra Topping, "Young musicians attract fan funding to avoid reliance on record industry", Guardian, 29 April 2012. http://www.guardian.co.uk/music/2012/apr/29/young-musicians-fan-funding-record-industry?CMP=twt_fd.
23. Quoted from an audio interview available online: Alex Blumberg, "An internet rock star tells all", NPR, 13 May 2011. http://www.npr.org/blogs/money/2011/05/14/136279162/an-internet-rock-star-tells-all?ft=1&f=1106.
24. http://www.jonathancoulton.com/wiki/Jonathan_Coulton.
25. Brenna Ehrlich, "Ben Folds on crowdfunding: 'We don't know what the f**k we're doing', O Music Blog, 11 May 2012. http://blog.omusicawards.com/2012/05/ben-folds-on-crowdfunding-we-dont-know-what-the-fk-were-doing/.
26. ibid.
27. Geoff Dyer, Out of Sheer Rage, p.129.
28. Gaston Bachelard, The Poetics of Space, p.6.
29. http://tumblr.ihatemornings.com/post/6283588322/im-pissed-off-about-the-press-not-the-news-press.

30. Hannah Nicklin, "'Music and theatre should belong to nobody, everybody' – Hannah Nicklin compares 'DIY' music with 'DIY' theatre", I Live Sweat, December 2011. http://ilivesweat.tumblr.com/post/13838799382/music-and-theatre-should-belong-to-nobody-everybody.

31. Alain de Botton, The Architecture of Happiness, p.25.

32. Paul Auster, Hand to Mouth (in Collected Prose, pp.153–4).

33. Christopher Small, Musicking: The Meanings of Performing and Listening, pp.8–9.

34. Derek Sivers, "Emphasize meaning over price = More paid sales", 21 September 2009. http://sivers.org/livecd.

35. David Bowie, "Tomorrow's rock'n'roll", Guardian, 15 January 1999. http://www.guardian.co.uk/technology/1999/jan/15/internet1.

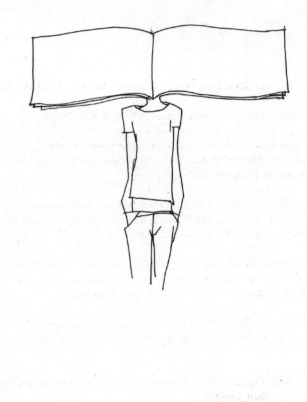

Bibliography

Auster, Paul (2003) *Collected Prose*, "Hand to Mouth". London: Faber and Faber.

Bachelard, Gaston (1994) *The Poetics of Space*. Boston: Beacon Press.

Barabbas, Louis (2012) "Musicians exposing themselves in public", *Louis Barabbas*, 12 July. Available at: http://louisbarabbas.com/articles/musicians-exposing-themselves-in-public/.

Blumberg, Alex (2011) "An internet rock star tells all", NPR, 13 May. Available at. http://www.npr.org/blogs/money/2011/05/14/136279162/an-internet-rock-star-tells-all?ft=1&f=1106.

Bogost, Ian (2012) "Kickstarter: crowdfunding platform or reality show?", *Fast Company*, 18 July. Available at: http://www.fastcompany.com/1843007/kickstarter-fundraising-or-a-new-kind-of-entertainment.

Bowie, David (1999) "Tomorrow's rock'n'roll", *Guardian*, 15 January [Online]. Available at: http://www.guardian.co.uk/technology/1999/jan/15/internet1.

Coulton, Jonathan (2012) *JoCopedia*. Available at: http://www.jonathancoulton.com/wiki/Jonathan_Coulton.

Crawford, Matthew (2009) *The Case for Working with Your Hands*. London: Viking.

de Botton, Alain (2007) *The Architecture of Happiness*. London: Penguin Books.

Dubber, Andrew (2012) *Music in the Digital Age*. Available at:
https://leanpub.com/dubber.

Dyer, Geoff (2009) *Out of Sheer Rage*. Great Britain: Abacus.

Egan, Jennifer (2011) *A Visit from the Goon Squad*. London: Corsair.

Ehrlich, Brenna (2012) "Ben Folds on crowdfunding: 'We don't know what the
f**k we're doing'", *O Music Awards*, 11 May. Available at: http://blog.
omusicawards.com/2012/05/ben-folds-on-crowdfunding-we-dont-know-what-
the-fk-were-doing/.

Grasmayer, Bas (2011) *The answer is the ecosystem: marketing music through non-linear
communication*. Thesis [Online]. Available at: http://basbasbas.com/thesis/.

— (2012) "Why music is not a product & three reasons why that's a good
thing", *Techdirt*, 14 February. Available at: http://www.techdirt.com/articles/
20120213/08223317744/why-music-is-not-product-three-reasons-why-
thats-good-thing.shtml.

Hersh, Kristin (2012) "Eden", *Kristin Hersh*, 26 January. Available at:
http://www.kristinhersh.com/eden/.

Jones, Sam (and agencies) (2012) "UK music sales decline for seventh
successive year despite downloads", *Guardian*, 2 January [Online]. Available at:
http://www.guardian.co.uk/music/2012/jan/02/uk-music-sales-decline-
2011.

Lakoff, George (2006) *Thinking Points*. New York: Farrar, Straus and Giroux.

Lawson, Steve (2009) "Independent music manifesto", *stevelawson.net*,
16 September. Available at: http://www.stevelawson.net/2009/09/
independent-music-manifesto/.

— (2012) "Every artist is a Kickstarter project", *stevelawson.net*, 14 February.
Available at: http://www.stevelawson.net/2012/02/every-artist-is-a-
kickstarter-project/#more-2890.

Letters of Note (2012) *You are mistaken in calling it a novel*. Available at: http://
www.lettersofnote.com/2012/03/you-are-mistaken-in-calling-it-novel.html.

Lynskey, Dorian (2012) "Leonard Cohen: 'All I've got to put in a song is my
own experience'", *Guardian*, 19 January [Online]. Available at: http://www.
guardian.co.uk/music/2012/jan/19/leonard-cohen.

Morris, William (2008) *Useful Work versus Useless Toil*. London: Penguin Books.

Nicklin, Hannah (2011) "'Music and theatre should belong to nobody, everybody' – Hannah Nicklin compares 'DIY' music with 'DIY' theatre", *I Live Sweat*, December. Available at: http://ilivesweat.tumblr.com/post/ 13838799382/music-and-theatre-should-belong-to-nobody-everybody.

Raisanen, Michael (2012) "The current rage in branding: fake authenticity is now a-okay", *Fast Company*, 15 March. Available at: http://www.fastcodesign. com/1669220/the-current-rage-in-branding-fake-authenticity-is-now-a-okay.

Ratcliffe, Sophie (ed.) (2011) *P.G.Wodehouse: A Life in Letters*. London: Hutchinson.

Ross, Alex (2011) *Listen to This*. London: Fourth Estate.

Sivers, Derek (2009) "Emphasize meaning over price = more paid sales", *Derek Sivers*, 21 September. Available at: http://sivers.org/livecd.

— (2010) "Seth Godin on spreading music and selling intimacy", *Derek Sivers*, 25 January. Available at: http://sivers.org/seth-godin.

Small, Christopher (1998) *Musicking*. Connecticut: Wesleyan University Press.

Topping, Alexandra (2012) "Young musicians attract fan funding to avoid reliance on record industry", *Guardian*, 29 April [Online]. Available at: http:// www.guardian.co.uk/music/2012/apr/29/young-musicians-fan-funding-record-industry?CMP=twt_fd.

Further Reading

These are books, essays, surveys, and other things that we like or looked at during the course of researching and writing this book. Just because something's on this list doesn't mean we necessarily agree with all of it, or endorse the views held by the authors – it just means we thought it was relevant or thought-provoking or funny or damn good.

Boeschenstein, Nell (2010) "Skills and Interests", *The Millions*, 20 May. Available at: http://www.themillions.com/2010/05/skills-and-interests.html.

Boesel, Whitney Erin (2012) "Music & control, or: why I keep arguing with my friends about Spotify", *Cyborgology*, 3 August. Available at: http://thesocietypages.org/cyborgology/2012/08/03/music-control-or-why-i-keep-arguing-with-my-friends-about-spotify/.

Cauty, Jimmy and Bill Drummond (1988) *The Manual (How to Have a Number One the Easy Way)*. KLF Publications.

Chayka, Kyle (2012) "eMPty3", *Bygone Bureau*, 30 July. Available at: http://bygonebureau.com/2012/07/30/empty3/.

Costello, Elvis (2011) "Steal this record", *Elvis Costello*, 18 November. Available at: http://www.elviscostello.com/news/steal-this-record/254.

Dawn, Nataly (2012) "Is Pomplamoose REALLY okay?", *Nataly Dawn Music*,

21 May. Available at: http://www.natalydawnmusic.com/2012/05/21/is-pomplamose-really-okay/.

Dyer, Geoff (2010) *But Beautiful*. Abacus.

Gill, Nick (2012) "Physical & digital & blah blah blah", *My Dreadful Career in Music*, 8 August. Available at: http://mydreadfulcareerinmusic.wordpress.com/2012/08/08/physical-digital-blah-blah-blah/.

Kidd, Laura (2011) "DIY music: what does it cost?", *She Makes War*, 15 October. Available at: http://shemakeswar.com/2011/10/15/diy-music-how-much/.

Kleon, Austin (2011) "Steal like an artist", *Austin Kleon*, 30 March. Available at: http://www.austinkleon.com/2011/03/30/how-to-steal-like-an-artist-and-9-other-things-nobody-told-me/.

Lanier, Jaron (2010) *You Are Not a Gadget*. London: Allen Lane.

Lewis, Craig (2011) "Funding for the benefit of Little Fish", 26 October. Available at: https://plus.google.com/104245907774547794896/posts/bhjVYA2TMhx.

Meyer, Robinson (2012) "How you turn music into money in 2012 (Spoiler: mostly iTunes)", *The Atlantic*, 3 August. Available at: http://www.theatlantic.com/technology/archive/2012/08/how-you-turn-music-into-money-in-2012-spoiler-mostly-itunes/260678/.

Salmon, Felix (2012) "Is Kickstarter selling dreams?", *Reuters*, 19 July. Available at: http://blogs.reuters.com/felix-salmon/2012/07/19/is-kickstarter-selling-dreams/.

Thomson, Kristin (2012) "Survey snapshot", *Artist Revenue Streams*, 8 February. Available at: http://money.futureofmusic.org/survey-snapshot/.

Verhoeve, Wesley (2012) "Louis CK's ticketing experiment (Or ticketing, this is how we do it)", *Wesley Verhoeve*, 26 June. Available at: http://www.wesleyverhoeve.com/louis-cks-ticketing-experiment-or-ticketing-this-is-how-we-do-it/.

Walker, Ben (2011) "We're gonna need a better myth", *Ben Walker (a musician)*, 13 December. Available at: http://tumblr.ihatemornings.com/post/14142223096/better-myth.

Acknowledgments

Over the course of writing this book, I've been helped and encouraged by countless friends, family members, and complete strangers, and I hope they all know how grateful I am.

In particular, I want to thank:

Louis Barabbas, Andrew Dubber, Bas Grasmayer, Steve Lawson, and Hannah Nicklin for granting me permission to quote from their work.

Gaz Coombes, Laura Kidd, Sophie Marfell, Robert Rosenberg, and Theo Whitworth for consenting to be interviewed and providing me with important perspectives as well as the opportunity to explore my own ideas through dialogue.

The team at Unbound, for being undaunted by my inexperience and willing to take this book on even before any of us really understood what it was all about.

Everyone who supported this book before it had even been written, without whom it simply wouldn't exist.

Ben Walker and Julia Heslop for their friendship, which has been so important, and for their unqualified willingness to participate in this funny little project.

My parents, Monte and Cynthia, for their unquestioning love and support, even from thousands of miles away and even when it hasn't been clear to any of us what I'm doing or where I'm headed.

My partner, Xander Cansell, for his apparently endless supply of love, encouragement, and patience, and for working tirelessly to ensure that this book got made.

– Miranda

Thank you to all my friends, family and fish fans who have kissed the sky so many times for us all. Miranda and Ben, thank you, you are both legends for even conceptualizing this book. Without you this book would never have existed. Miranda, I hope one day you don't have to live on the bread line to fund your art, you are so talented so keep writing and don't let your heart give out. Thank you to Ben, without you, I would be nothing, thank you for speaking my kind of soul, music and heart. I kinda love you. Thank you to Xander, you took all of our hearts and sold this book to Unbound. You helped drag our shadows to the sun. Thank you Bekim Mala, Becks, Becky, Speckle Hen, you are a genius. I'm always falling in love with your crazy artistic ideas, thank you for designing the cover to this book. Thank you Nez, you who spent years by my side. We both foolishly believed. I will always feel your absence. Thank you to my mother, I'm not sure this book would ever have got funded without you, luckily for us you are a great emailer. Thank you also to all you supporters who have watched us over the years, who've got up and turned on the sound of our record and pledged for our crazy book. You really do believe in us. Thank you to Candy Says – Ben, Elisa and Mike – who have been there for me, who have helped take Little Fish safely out of the water only to keep memories. It's too late for music to make us feel sad again. It's too late for music to make me feel sad again.

– Juju

Subscribers

Unbound is a new kind of publishing house. Our books are funded directly by readers. This was a very popular idea during the late eighteenth and early nineteenth century. Now we have revived it for the internet age. It allows authors to write the books they really want to write and readers to support the writing they would most like to see published.

The names listed below are of readers who have pledged their support and made this book happen. If you'd like to join them, visit: www.unbound.co.uk.

Zita Abila

Jennifer Acton

Warble Entertainment Agency

Richard Aitken

Neil Anderson

Nathan Archer

Paul Askew

Eliane Aubain

Sasha Bach

David Balch

Mark Baldwin

Natalie Banner

Gilberte Bansillon

Spencer Barden

Helen Barker

John & Béatrice Barnet

Niki Beavon

Charlotte Bennett

Julie Bennett

Maxine Berg

A Little Bird

Corinne Birken

Derek Blackham

Phil Blaney

Kit Boise-Cossart

Vreni Booth

Sandra Boreham

Patricia Borrows

Debby Boulton

Nathan Boyce

Liz Branson

Richard W H Bray

Grant Brereton

Alessandro Briganti

Brian Briggs

Hannah Bruce

Kriss Buddle

Val Bullock

Monika Bulsiewicz

Cecile Bultingaire

Vinny Burke

Jean Burrell

Natalie Bushnell

Richard Butchins

Michael Butterworth

Iain Cadman

David Callier

Brian Cameron

Ed Cansell

Jill & Peter Cansell

Xander Cansell

Brenda Cantu

Mick & Jane Carling

Paul Carrera

Steve Carter

Francoise Chegne

Laura Clark

Oliver Clark

Garrett Coakley

Josh Cobb

Laurence Colbert

Sean Collins

Tania Collyer

Cookie & Asia

Gina Cowen

Jo Cox

Cheryl Craig

John Creavy

Rich Cross

Angela Da Costa

Chris Dalton

Nick Darbyshire

Tony Davis

Simon Dawes

Robert Day

Lykle de Vries

Ben Denison

Michelle Denny

Anna Di Stefano

Charles Dickens

Ian Dickson

Maja Dierenfeld

Deborah Donne

Natalie Dorey

Fionnuala Dorrity

Ruairi Dorrity

Liliane Doumèche

Elizabeth Dray

Siobhán Dudleston

Emily Duffy

Michel Dumontet

Janice Duquenoy

John Edwards

Karen Egan

Richard Elkington

David Emery

Richard Evans

Charles Fernyhough

Mike Fitzgerald

Jennifer Fleming

Clementine Ford

Elisabeth Fraser

Debbie Frayling

John Frewin

Finlay Games

Sue Garland

Louis Gereaux

Cyrus Gilbert-Rolfe

Brian & Yvonne Gill

Nick Gill

Paul Gill

Vickie Gill

Katja Glies

Dave Goater

Sophie Goldsworthy

Dominic Graham-Hyde

Summer Grant

Bas Grasmayer (@Spartz)

Tony Gray

Tom Greeves

Alan Griffiths

Cathy Griffiths

David Griffiths

Hailey Grimes

Paul Gullis

Adam Gurr

Samantha Hall

Louise Harris

Jill & Adrian Hartless

Lee Hartwell

Steve Hay

Daren Headley

Frederick Hedd

Rachael Hemsley

Vince Henry

Annemarie Heslop

Tony Heslop

Lynsey Hester

George Hickman

Christa Hillhouse

Sean Hodgson

Katharina Howard

Barrie Howe

Phil Hudson

Robin Hurley

Cathy Hurren

Ali Hussain

Chiara Iacobazzi

Sylvie Jacquet-Francillon

Steve Jalim

Fadi Jameel

Dan 'Mr Pumpkinhead' James

Jay James

Ania Jayne

Angharad Jenkins

Brennig Jones

Dylan Jones

Kurt Jones

Smith Jones

Alexa Jury

Nicole Kaeuper

Keith Kahn-Harris

Andrew Katz

Janet Keene

Laura Kidd

Dan Kieran

Dave Kirkham

Caroline Knight

Nick Koonce
Gabor Kovacs
Robert Krczal
Tarn Lake
Oleg Lavrovsky
Jason Le Page
Laura Le Rox
Jonathan Lee
Charlie Lee-Potter
Paul Lenz
Craig Lewis
Erica Lewis
Jennifer Lowerre
George Lutz
Anita M
Philippe & Jean-Paul Macaigne
Ketan Majmudar
Lucy Marfell
Paul Marfell
Sophie Marfell
Tom Marfell
Richard Markham
Charlotte Martine
Ash Matadeen
Ciaran Matthews
Ed Matthews
Elisabeth Matthews
Francis Matthews
Sophie McAllister
Andrew McCluskey
Andrew McCrorie-Shand
Robert McIntosh
Stuart McKears
Emma McMenamy
Chris McVeigh
Rachel Meir

Ian Melton
Andrew Milloy
Ginestra Ferraro & Paola Mirra
John Mitchinson
Ty Moffett
Andrew Morris
Sean Morris
Treana Morris
Kate Mosse
Dave Motion
Sami Mughal
Anthony Murphy
Becca Murphy
Tricia (Shabby Pots) Murphy
Tim Myatt
Andy Nichol
Zachary Noel
Stephen O'Brien
Sharon Oates
Andrew Ogilvy
Andrew Palmer
Tamara Parsons-Baker
Marc Pastowsky
Laura Peach
Josette Penner
Alan Phillips
Kate Pincock
Louise Pocock
Justin Pollard
Rachel Poulton
Adrian Pratt
Johnny Pugsley
Gary Pyke
Frank Ralph
Sophie Ratcliffe
Stuart Reilly

Claudia Ricciardi

Alissa Robinson

Izzy Rodriguez

Luca Rondanini

Cormac Ross

Shay Rowan

Sandrine Ruitton

Vicky Russell

Ruth Ryan

Kris Sangani

Derya Erdem Sarac

Michael Scammell

Ruth Scott

Alan Searl

Tina Sheikh

Martin Sissons

Paul Skinner

Alasdair Smith

Carey Snowden

Nick Speller

Alison Stallard

K C Still

Abi Stone

Paul Swinbank

Garrick T

Dror Tankus

Daniel Tarrare

Shaun Taylor

Damian Thomas

Georgia Blue Townshend

Tim & Ro Turan

Naomi Turnbull

Amy Utley

Samuele Valerio

Petrus & Sarah van der Westhuizen

Donalda Wain

Steve Wain

Jennifer Walker

John Walker

Paul Walker

Shraddha & Adrian Walker

Spencer Walker

Caroline Wallace

Joanna Walsh

Cynthia Carbone Ward

Lisa Ward

Monte R Ward

Nancy & Monte Ward

Cara Waterfall

Angela Waterhouse

Anne Watson

David Wells

Robert Wells

Ben Werdmuller

Gail Wernham

Matt Westcott

Lee Westmoreland

Sarah Westwood

Clyde Whitham

Jont Whittington

Theo Whitworth

Olly Willans

Vincent Winter

Jenny Woods

Alwyn Woolley

Ronelli Yeats

Alan Yentob

Elisa Zoot

@supportlf